A
LIGHT
ON THE
CORNER

ALSO BY ANDREA RAYNOR

The Voice That Calls You Home: Inspiration for Life's Journeys

Incognito: Lost and Found at Harvard Divinity School

The Choice

ANDREA RAYNOR

A
LIGHT
ON THE
CORNER

Discovering the
Sacred in the Everyday

Waterfall
PRESS

Published by Waterfall Press, Grand Haven, MI
www.brilliancepublishing.com

Amazon, the Amazon logo, and Waterfall Press are trademarks of Amazon.com,
Inc., or its affiliates.

Scriptures taken from the Holy Bible, New International Version®, NIV®. Copyright
© 1973, 1978, 1984, 2011 by Biblica, Inc.™ Used by permission of Zondervan. All
rights reserved worldwide. www.zondervan.com The "NIV" and "New International
Version" are trademarks registered in the United States Patent and Trademark Office
by Biblica, Inc.™

Scripture quotations marked (ESV) are from the ESV® Bible (The Holy Bible,
English Standard Version®), copyright © 2001 by Crossway, a publishing ministry of
Good News Publishers. Used by permission. All rights reserved.

ISBN-13: 9781503943407
ISBN-10: 1503943402

Cover design by Joan Wong

Printed in the United States of America

For my parents,
Richard and Lillian Ruehrwein,
who taught me how to see life
as a spiritual adventure

Open your eyes and the whole world is full of God.

—*Jakob Böhme*

CONTENTS

The Prize

Standing at the kitchen sink, I gaze out at the familiar patch of earth that is my backyard. Birds sing, leaves flutter gently in the breeze, a squirrel hangs upside down from a branch. It is an insignificant everyday moment, one of an endless stream that makes up the minutes and hours, days and years of our lives. It is not noteworthy. It is not exciting—and yet it is inherently mystical. For right here and now, amid my dog's snores and the passing of cars, amid dishes in the sink and bills on the table, exists the possibility of experiencing mystery, of glimpsing the Divine.

I sink into my chair at the table and think about this again. Do I truly believe it is possible to have a genuine encounter with the Holy? On good days, of course I do. But even spiritual people, religious people—like myself—can have moments of doubt. Images of all the sadness in the world fill my mind: hungry children, war-torn countries, families in crisis, natural disasters. At first glance it makes more sense to argue *against* the existence of the Divine than to argue for it. Perhaps our hunger for connection to something greater than ourselves is but a flimsy defense to keep our loneliness and our fear of death at bay. Believing there is more to life than meets the eye gives us a toehold in the scheme of things. It gives us hope and inspires us to persevere in the search for meaning. Some would say that we infuse the events that happen in our lives with magical thinking, that there is no such thing as God or Spirit or an authentic mystical experience. I am familiar with these arguments. I know it is irrational and perhaps anti-intellectual for me to believe in God—but from deep within rumbles an undeniable and stubborn *Yes!* Yes to life, yes to mystery, yes to the possibility of transcendence.

Believing is one thing. How to actually experience the spiritual as we go about our days presents a challenge. I wish there were a surefire recipe, a *Five Easy Steps* to encountering the Divine. Then again, maybe I don't. It is the seeking that keeps our spirits lean and hungry, the not-knowing that keeps us moving. The questions with which I grapple on a continual basis are my spiritual sit-ups. Is God inspiration or incarnation? Is God unknowable, or one of us, as the singer Joan Osborne once pondered? And if God *were* one of us, would we be disappointed? Perhaps it would be like searching for a king and finding, instead, a baby in a manger.

Even for those of us who naturally ponder such questions, trying to discern a path of spiritual integrity can be confusing and frustrating. Although we are desperate to connect with that which is beyond ourselves, many of us don't know how to go about it, and if we do, how can we be sure of the authenticity of our experiences? *Show me a sign,* we ask the Universe in our times of struggle or quiet meditation. And just when it seems we've been talking to ourselves, the phone rings, carrying the familiar voice of a friend, a hawk startles us with its beauty as it spreads its wings in flight, or we see a shooting star flash across the night sky like a match ignited. *Coincidence,* we wonder, *or divine message? Interruption, or answer to prayer?* How do we tell the difference between what is an authentic spiritual experience and what is not, what is imagination and what belongs to the realm of Mystery?

Sometimes reaching for the Divine feels like trying to grasp liquid mercury in our bare hands. Even if we see it, we're not sure how to handle it—and this scares us. I remember once when I was a child watching the silver bead of mercury escape from a broken thermometer.

It slid across the bathroom floor as if alive—elusive and menacing, fascinating and alluring. "Don't touch that!" warned my mother, the sharp caution in her voice instantly riveting me to the spot. The bead came to rest in a corner by the tub, a miniature alien looking defiant against the pink tile and pulsating with wild, dangerous possibility. *Only my mother knows how to handle mercury,* I thought. How strange to think that a moment ago, it had been in my mouth, separated from my tongue by a thin piece of glass. Encased, we took it for granted. Exposed, it was a tiny atomic bomb.

Perhaps we need the thin veil of unknowability that separates us from the Divine. Perhaps, revealed, it would be too much for us to bear—the beauty, the light, the truth of all that is. As the psalmist wrote so long ago, "Such knowledge is too wonderful for me, too lofty for me to attain".[1] As very human beings, we are not ready to see the totality of the Spirit; we could not bear to hold the Divine, unfiltered, in our hands. Holiness is the most primordial of elements; it is inextricably bound to the created world, infusing all that is, all that can be known, and all that remains a mystery. This spiritual reality permeates existence. It is encoded in our DNA. It is living energy, which, like gravity, does not rely on our ability to see or touch or taste it; it simply is. When we accept this fact, accept our limited ability to perceive that which exists just beyond our human senses, then we may begin to notice the bits and particles of the Divine that are safely at hand.

We can hold mercury, but only if it is encased in glass; we can touch the Divine, but only if it is embedded in the created world. Even at a great distance, the sun burns our eyes when we look directly at it—but we can taste it in a strawberry or see it in the green of a leaf. So, too, we could not bear direct contact with the One who made the sun, but we can feel the warmth of the Creator in the embrace of our loved ones. Meister Eckhart, the thirteenth-century mystic and theologian, said

---

1   Psalm 139:6, New International Version.

something like, *If you stare at the sun long enough, you will see, for a time, the image of the sun wherever you look.* Likewise, if we look at God long enough, we will see the image of God everywhere and in everything.

The idea that God's presence is a visible, accessible reality, that our days are saturated with opportunities to experience the mystical, may sound like wishful thinking. Perhaps this is because many of us are hoping for something dramatic—the winning lottery ticket, the healing of a loved one—before we surrender our skepticism. *Then I'd believe*, we tell ourselves. And we go along pretty well until something happens in our lives that throws us rather unexpectedly into the existential wrestling arena. When we land, it can be very difficult to know where and to whom we can turn to find answers that we can live with. If we were to believe religious extremists—of any faith—the path to God is very narrow. And if the television evangelists are right, most of us are in real danger of going to hell.

This thought is in stark contrast to something I heard a Catholic priest say years ago to a group of hospice workers. He had been a priest in the prison system, serving inmates who had committed terrible crimes—murder, rape, armed robbery. When asked about his view on eternal life and whether everyone goes to heaven, he paused, an imperceptible sigh escaping his lips. I watched him anxiously, having been put on the spot myself a time or two by colleagues or patients who suspected my theology was too broad and open armed. I noticed his eyes were warm and forgiving but there was something else there, too: courage, integrity, and the heat of a burning faith churning like molten lava from deep within. Looking out at his small audience, he said with a soft, gentle voice, "Since I have yet to meet a person whom God could not forgive, I do not believe in hell."

As we go about our lives, the great majority of us are neither egregious sinners nor perfect saints. We are merely created people doing the best we can, sometimes stumbling, sometimes shining, and sometimes crying out like lost lambs for the reassurance that God exists, that life goes on, and that we have not been left orphaned and abandoned on this little planet. This yearning prompts many of us to look for signs that Someone is listening and that our prayers for guidance are being heard. My best friend swears she receives messages through people's license plates. She is someone who spends her life in dialogue with the Divine, so it makes sense that, sitting at a traffic light or parking her car, words or initials that mean something will pop out to her. One could say that she reads into things, that she creates her own meaning, but maybe, because she is open to such things, the answers appear. For others, especially for those who are hurting, the heavens seem stubbornly silent. Often we yearn for meaning but feel only despair. When left too long to our own devices, we come up with a thousand reasons why there could be no God, no higher meaning, no purpose to our lives. Little do we know that the reassurance we seek is hidden like a treasure in plain sight.

I first learned this lesson many years ago when I was a child, no more than six or seven years old. It was Easter, and our neighbors were hosting a giant multifamily egg hunt at their house. The sun was warm and the ground was soft with new green grass just beginning to push its way out of the damp earth. The small strawberry patch in their field had yet to be planted, but it still looked friendly and inviting, holding the promise of summer. Even the trees, with their tiny buds, looked like old friends who'd just gotten home from a long trip and had yet to unpack their bags.

We children were still in our Sunday best, baskets slung over our arms, when we lined up on the patio to hear instructions. As one of the mothers outlined the perimeter of the hunt, my heart pounded with excitement. I could see the other children already eyeing the eggs that were close at hand and clearly in view, plotting their strategies, deciding which way to run first. The last thing the mother told us was that in addition to the regular candy and eggs, there was one grand prize, different from the others, unusual and special—and immediately it was what all of us wanted most. She did not tell us what it was, only that we would know it when we saw it.

Someone blew a whistle and we were off in a flash, fanning out into the backyard. We must have looked like giant frogs as we ran and stopped, ran and stopped, squatting down to snatch up eggs from the grass, then springing back up again. Children poked along the fence, moving rocks and squealing whenever two reached for the same treasure. After most of the treats were discovered, we had to move more slowly, looking more carefully for any lingering booty. Soon the older children's baskets were full, a testimony to their greater speed and savvy, but even the youngest weren't faring too poorly. Still, the grand prize had yet to be found.

I remember walking slowly with my basket, a feeling of happiness enveloping me as I scanned the grass for stragglers. Finding none, I decided to make my way back to the patio. As I walked along I raised my eyes to the sky, letting the early spring sun warm my face. Then, as I passed a large bush, I saw it. Funny thing is, I wasn't even looking for it. But there it was, in plain view for all to see. I stopped in my tracks and stared, thinking I must be seeing things. A large white plastic bunny sat, barely hidden, in a bush that had yet to bud. It was about a foot tall, with pretty blue eyes and a demure expression. Realistic in shape and design, not cartoonish, it looked to me like the guardian angel of bunnies. Instinctively, I looked around, swiveling my head from side to side, thinking another child would surely come at any moment to snatch the prize from my grasp, but there was no one in sight. My hands shook a little as I reached and gently retrieved her from the branches of the bush. Her weight and the rustle in her belly told me that she was stuffed with candy. But the candy wasn't what filled me with awe. Holding the bunny in my hands, I felt like I was holding something otherworldly, that I was holding magic, that somehow God had looked down at me and smiled. We had a secret, and the secret was that I was loved.

When I returned to the patio with the plastic bunny, the mothers smiled. "Oh, look who found the grand prize!" Some of the other children gathered around, cooing, asking to hold her, asking where I had found her. "She was just sitting in that bush," I said, pointing. "Sitting right there, not even hidden at all." How no one had discovered her, I could not fathom. We had all run by that spot a thousand times.

Sometimes the simplest of experiences can remind us that we are loved by God. God didn't place that bunny in the bush, but my six-year-old self interpreted it in a spiritual way. This is what made the experience authentic. Someone else may not have had the same feeling I did about finding that treasure, and maybe it sounds incredibly insignificant, but for me it was profound. Suddenly God's presence was tangible. It was tactile. I could hold it in my hands. It had been there all along, quietly observing me as I darted about. And it had revealed itself in a blue-sky moment when I had given up searching.

The feeling that I experienced something mystical in the discovery of that treasure has stayed with me. It may not have been a miracle—a burning bush or an apparition—but it left me with an early awareness of encountering the Holy. The fantastical or miraculous nature of our experiences matters less than the deep feelings they invoke. Perhaps this is the miracle: allowing ourselves to be open to the possibility that God is in our midst, and then experiencing the Divine buried in the mundane. In the end, it is the stirring of the heart that matters—that's where God resides.

For those who seek to know the Spirit, or yearn to have a spiritual experience, the best place to start is in our routine days. Of this I am convinced. If it were not so, then the mystical would belong only to an elite group of seers: to prophets and poets, to healers and holy men, to intuitives and those who have visions. Few of us will wrestle with an angel as Jacob did, much less part the waters of the sea. And if we did, would we have the humility and grace to recognize that it is God who empowers us, surrounds us, and ignites our aspiration? It is common to yearn for a dramatic spiritual experience—and then doubt it when one has transpired. How many times have I heard the anguished cry of the bereaved to see a loved one again, while remaining blindfolded by tears, by doubt, and by a stubborn refusal to acknowledge the possibility of angels in their midst?

We are not alone in life. Most of us know this somewhere deep down, even if we are afraid to trust it, much less say it out loud. We may not see the angels around us, but we can discover the traces they have left behind, evidence of the unexplainable. Perhaps we need to crack the doors of our hearts open, just a tiny bit, as we stand at our kitchen windows or sit at our desks or walk along the streets. In doing so, we invite the Spirit into our lives. And when that guest arrives, the experience can be akin to suddenly seeing the world around us like a double exposure. Our physical eyes will see the familiar shapes, but our inner vision, our creative insight, will see remnants of the Spirit, the infusion of divine energy, swirling and pulsating in every moment.

Our lives are a collection of moments in which we can see God's thumbprint. Each experience is a star in our constellation; each helps light our way and chart our course. When I feel lost, I think of the stories in my life and I can begin to find my way back to the path. Our stories are like celestial bread crumbs: they tell us who we are and where we've been. They point toward mystery. We can look at our lives and see a one-dimensional painting, a mundane list of dates and events, or we can search for the stardust buried there. If stories were stars, they would form a sparkling mosaic, unique to each individual but burning with the same bright light, the patterns continuously mingling and merging. We could point to them and say, "Oh, this is where I fell in love" or "This is where my heart broke, and this is where it healed." We could see the beauty inherent in our days and marvel at the intricacies that have made us who we are.

Before we toss our stories to the heavens for safekeeping, however, we must live them. Each moment presents an opportunity to experience the sacred and to reach for what is only thinly veiled. We don't have to know what we are looking for—in fact most of us don't have an inkling—all that is required is that we show up. We bring our tattered selves, we bring our Sunday best; we try not to shove the other children, we occasionally remember to turn our faces to the sun. The Divine is not "out there" somewhere waiting to be found; our loved ones are not "up there" somewhere far from us. These flimsy boundaries are of our own making because we simply cannot fathom the intimacy and the immediacy of God's presence.

Each of us has already won the prize. We are created beings, loved by the Creator, connected by the continuum of Spirit and time. If we allow ourselves to see the world as inherently mystical, each moment can be one of meaning and discovery. Then there will be no yearning for God, for we will see God in everything. There will be no loneliness, for we will know that we are never alone.

Blood Orange

The first thing I noticed was the aroma. It arrived lightly, like a whisper or a passing thought, just perceptible enough to turn one's head. I imagined myself being lifted by my nose and floating in a dreamlike state on an invisible cloud of sweetness. I searched for its source through the gray-blue wall of people who swayed in synchronized rhythm, blocking my view. The subway car was crowded with afternoon travelers, many of them students riding the city equivalent of a school bus. Despite the packed car, it was strangely quiet thanks to the personal force fields generated by iPods, tablets, and cell phones. Glancing around, I noticed that almost every head was bowed as people stared into their devices—our modern-day version of prayer.

When the doors opened at the next station, a load of people got out, finally affording me a view across the aisle. It was then that I spotted a small boy about five years old. He was sitting with legs dangling and feet, just shy of being able to reach the floor, crossed comfortably at the ankles. His hands were folded loosely in his lap; every muscle looked relaxed. Because he was not looking at me, I was able to study him quietly and without apology. His beautiful round face, the color of a creamy latte, appeared neither excited nor disinterested. In fact, his expression defied easy categorizing, which was part of what I found so intriguing. The best I could come up with was that it resonated with an oddly patient trust. He was a miniature Buddha living totally in the moment.

Sitting next to him was a teenage girl. Too young to be his mother, she must have been his sister, or so I assumed. Her expression was similar to that of the boy's: still, without being particularly happy or sad. At first glance one could mistake it for boredom, but boredom does not captivate. It was as if the two of them were on the train utterly alone; as if there were no stops, no stations, and nowhere to be or to go.

In the girl's hands was a large orange, an orb of color amid the drab backdrop. Each puncture of her nails into its skin sent a ripple of freshness through the train car, the kind that makes your mouth water, the kind that makes you long for a taste. I noticed other passengers drawing deep, secret breaths as if surreptitiously trying to sneak off with some of it, but the subtle expansion of their nostrils gave them away. It was the smell of summer, of life; it was a reminder of a world beyond technology and concrete. A smile crept across my face before I could reel it back in.

My eyes drifted from face to face, from the inhaling bliss of the passengers to the stillness of the children, until it came to rest on the hands of the young girl. Her fingers were long and slender and lithe. Like the legs of a spider, they moved with delicate agility, steadily working their way around the orange. They were the type of hands that poets write about or painters try to capture—hands that should be held gently, like a five-petal flower.

Once the thick outer peel had been removed, the girl placed it carefully on a napkin in her lap. Naturally, I thought that the dance was concluding, that the spell would be broken, the orange eaten, and the hands that moved so beautifully around it would lose their magic, the way things do when the clock strikes twelve. The subway car would no longer be Cinderella's fragrant carriage; it would be an ordinary pumpkin, and the girl would be just another teenager heading home after school with her little brother in tow. To my surprise, however, the story was just beginning. Instead of splitting the orange open and popping a section into her mouth, she began the tedious job of removing all the remaining white strands from the orange. *All* of them. I watched in awe as her tapered fingers methodically went about their work. The orange was a small, fragile world in her hands. She was completely focused, holding it, turning it, and gently removing the bits of debris left by the peel. With each passing moment its perfection was emerging. It was like watching a sculpture being released from its marble tomb with each chisel by the artist. I wondered how long she would work at it; at what point would she be satisfied, and what would she do when at last she finished her masterpiece?

I considered my own impatience. The way I rush through my life, the way I am more likely to grab a quick bite of something than to savor it, the way I have a tendency to accept when things are "good enough" rather than aspiring to perfection. This girl was in no rush. Each strand that she pulled off the orange was like her first. What's more, her little brother accepted this. He did not tug at her sleeve. He did not even speak. *Maybe he doesn't like oranges,* I reasoned.

As each stop came and went along the subway line, I began to worry that I would have to get off before knowing the end of the story. *Even if my stop comes,* I thought, *I'm not moving.* I was transfixed. And I realized that I was not alone. Others, too, had raised their eyes from their devices to watch the beautiful fingers. *She has the hands of a surgeon,* I thought. *She has the hands of God,* I heard from somewhere else.

I watched as she turned the orange in her hands and held it up to her eyes for examination. It was flawless. Without a shred of residue remaining, it appeared illuminated from within. While her movements indicated that she might finally be satisfied, her expression had not changed. She was still unreadable, a creamy palette upon which the rest of us could project our interpretations and feelings.

She carefully split the orange into two perfect halves, then separated one of those halves into yet a smaller section. At that point, I fully expected her to simply start eating it. Instead, in a gesture filled with effortless grace, she handed that slice of perfection to the little boy. *It was never for her at all,* I realized, *the effort, the meticulous care. This whole time it was for her brother.* As the train continued from station to station, the girl never tasted a single piece of what she had created. Instead, she just kept handing sections to the child, who received them in his small open palms and brought them to his lips.

I relaxed until my stop finally came, knowing that the beauty of the scene had moved me but not fully understanding why. On the surface, one could say that this was just a teenager on a crowded train, peeling an orange for a little boy. She peeled, he ate, no big deal. But what it looked like, what it felt like, was communion. She would not serve him until the perfection of the host was revealed. Nothing else would do. He might have settled for less—he was probably too young to know the difference—but *she* knew. And her presence, one of trustworthy authority and beauty, conveyed that it was worth the wait. Something promised would be given when the time was ripe, but not until then. As for the boy, he seemed to know that her effort was for him and him alone; hence the waiting was peaceful and free of worry. There was no fidgeting, no impatience—just surrendered synchronicity.

Can an orange be the blood of Christ? This question was actually posed to me by a chaplain when I was in college. In truth, it wasn't something that he wanted to know my thoughts on, but rather a rhetorical question aimed to mock and shame me. Before I could speak, he responded with a resounding, outraged *"No."* And that *no* effectively ended my participation in the Christian Fellowship on campus and in any activities that particular chaplain might be leading. It also left a scar on the part of my heart that got caught when he slammed the door on it.

It was the beginning of my senior year at Denison. Many students, myself included, were back on campus after having studied elsewhere during their junior year. I had just returned from a spring semester in Vienna, while my friend Chris had spent the semester at the University of Michigan. Not only had we roomed together before setting off on our journeys, but we were also friends who shared a faith. Chris was quiet, smart, and a solid friend. I trusted her opinions and I valued the way we could share our struggles and our spirituality. She was the only friend at Denison I ever prayed with or—as far as I knew—read the Bible without having to do so for a class.

We were barely settled into our dorms when we learned that a new Dean of Religious Life had been hired. Since both of us had been involved in the Christian Fellowship throughout the previous three years, and since I was one of only six senior religion majors, we thought it'd be nice to make a visit to the new dean to welcome him. It seemed the hospitable thing to do, especially since the Christian community was rather small—or at least very low key—at that time.

We were in good spirits, feeling cheerful and open as we climbed the stairs to the dean's office. A broad, lumpy man in his late thirties or early forties stood to greet us. He had a closely cropped beard and thinning brown hair that was brushed carefully across his head. We shook hands and introduced ourselves, then he motioned for us to settle into a couple of leather chairs opposite his desk. As we chatted, I remember being slightly underwhelmed by his response to our friendly overture. He emitted a cool formality that dropped like a Plexiglas wall between us. I don't think he could yet appreciate how rare this type of spontaneous visit would be for him. Most of our fellow students were more interested in throwing a Frisbee, blasting the Dead, or tapping a keg that first week back at school. I couldn't think of anyone else who would be seeking out the dean to say hello.

In the interest of making conversation, or building a connection with him, I decided to share an experience I'd had during my recent time abroad. Perhaps I wanted to illustrate the depth of my spirituality as a way of gaining his trust, or maybe we were just floundering for things to say. In either case, it felt like we needed a spiritual can opener to pry open his steely heart, and I thought this story might do it.

"So, I had this incredible experience on Crete," I began. My stomach was rather queasy, which should have been an indication that I should *stop right there*, but it was too late.

"Really," he said, from a distance that felt much further away than the width of his desk.

"Yes," I replied, trying to sound cheerful and breezy, though my mouth had gone a bit dry and the Sahara Desert was suddenly filling my throat. I glanced at Chris, who smiled and nodded in an encouraging way, though in retrospect, her hands were clasped just a little too tightly in her lap.

I proceeded to describe to him how my roommate, Andrea, and I had decided to travel from Vienna to Greece during our spring break. We were on a shoestring budget (well, I was anyway) but the rail ticket wasn't too expensive and we planned on camping or staying in youth hostels. The local train from Vienna to Athens took almost forty hours, the bulk of which we were forced to stand because there were no available seats. Although slightly alarmed at the nonchalant overcrowding of the train—it felt like an accident waiting to happen—we just climbed on board and went with it. We spent the first thirty hours of the trip standing in the long, narrow hallway outside of the enclosed compartments. Balancing on our backpacks or trying to sit on the floor, we had to move every time one of the compartment doors opened or someone wanted to pass by. Needless to say, it was exhausting. It's no wonder, then, that when we were finally offered a seat, we readily took it, despite the questionable conditions of the offer.

The night had been rough but relatively quiet. In the morning, however, the train was alive with activity. People were squeezing and pushing past us in a continual stream to make their way to the bathroom or simply to stretch their legs. Various languages mingled in the air, rising like bird songs in the forest—distinct, beautiful, comical. Sometimes Andrea and I spoke to each other in German, other times in English, and sometimes all we needed was a look. The look on that particular morning said, "Don't talk to me unless you can find coffee."

The day wore on and minutes tumbled into hours. We had stopped noticing the people who passed, so we were rather startled when a young man sidled up next to us. He was slim and well dressed, with neatly styled black hair and beautiful dark-olive skin. In halting English, he said that he might be able to offer us a seat in his cabin in exchange for a small favor. Andrea, a native New Yorker, shot me a look that meant *Don't open your mouth*, then she rolled her eyes. We might have been tired but we weren't complete idiots. At the same time, both of us became acutely aware of the ache in our legs and backs. Our hesitation must have revealed a crack in our resolve because the man began to wave us on with the smooth enthusiasm of a snake oil salesman. We looked at each other, shrugged, and then followed him down the corridor.

The glass door to his compartment slid open, revealing four other smiling, smooth-skinned men. "Come in! Come in!" they said jovially, making room for us on the benched seats that faced one another. Our antennas went up but it felt *so good* to sit down. Even though we knew there must be a catch to their friendliness, we did not feel in danger. One of the men offered us water as another explained their dilemma. Apparently, they had several packages of, ahem, *coffee* that they were trying to get home but needed help carrying. If we would be so kind as to stuff some of the bundles in our packs, they would repay us by sharing their compartment. Then, as if to reassure us, they opened one of the packages to reveal its contents: coffee. Sigh.

Against our better judgment, we agreed. Bundles were jammed into our backpacks in exchange for seats, water, cheese, and fruit. When the conductor came by for our tickets, it appeared as if we were all old friends. It's possible that I imagined his suspicious gaze, but I was relieved all the same when he left without incident. When we pulled into Athens, our impromptu traveling companions retrieved their packages, and we all went on our merry ways. I shudder to think what else was in those bundles or what might have happened had we gotten caught with them. "That was pretty stupid," Andrea and I agreed. "Let's not do that again."

Two days later, we found ourselves on the island of Crete. The youth hostel sat atop a mountain overlooking the sea. We slept under the stars in bunk beds that were lined up in rows on the roof, filled mostly with young people from various parts of Europe. It was quite magical. We didn't give another thought to the long train ride or to our mysterious acquaintances. Instead, we ate fresh yogurt with honey, we jogged a few miles down the mountain each day to the beach, we sipped ouzo and danced with the locals at night.

On the third morning I woke before dawn, aware that it was Easter—not Orthodox Easter but Easter for many other Christians, including those back home. I had asked Andrea the night before if she would like to join me for a walk in the morning to meditate, but she politely declined. Andrea was culturally Jewish but not religious. I'd figured she wouldn't be interested, but I didn't want her to worry if she woke to find me gone.

The sky was an illuminated indigo as I quietly slipped out of my sleeping bag; the air and the ground were damp with the morning dew. After pulling on my shoes, I stood for a moment looking out from our perch. The orange-gold rays of the sun had yet to break the surface of the water but the horizon was beginning to glow. I tucked my pocket-size New Testament into my jacket and began wandering down the mountain in search of a place to pray. Although I was alone on the road, I did not feel alone because I knew that other Christians were preparing for their own sunrise services. The same sun would wake them; the same story would inspire them. I was part of a global community.

Suddenly, I felt a desire to participate in a communion of sorts, one that would solidify and symbolize my connection to the body of Christ in the world. With this in mind, I wandered down into the small village not far from the hostel. It was comprised of only a few shops, all of which were still shuttered and dark. Disappointed, I started on my way when one of the doors opened. A friendly looking man (clearly surprised to see me there) greeted me in Greek. Using gestures and words I did not recognize, he seemed to be asking if there was anything I needed, despite the fact that his shop wasn't yet open for business. I tried to convey that I wanted to buy grape juice and bread. Scratching his balding head, he offered me a bottle of orange soda and some vanilla wafers instead. Whether he didn't understand what I wanted or whether this was all he had wasn't important. I was happy with what he gave me and grateful that he had opened the door.

I continued down the mountain path, which was getting steeper and more rugged with each step. Meanwhile, the sun was making its dramatic entrance, commanding the sky as though it were a giant stage. If beams of light were sound, the world would have been bathed in a symphony too beautiful to describe. As it was, the singing of the birds and the whisper of the breeze provided the only accompaniment of the morning: nature's Easter hymn. And that was enough.

When I was about halfway between the sea and the youth hostel, I turned off the path and found a big rock upon which to sit. Breathing deeply, I shut my eyes and turned my face to the sky. I pictured my mother and father rising to sing "Christ the Lord Is Risen Today" in our Methodist Church in Cincinnati, their voices blending with their neighbors', blending with *their* neighbors', blending with the great chorus of Christians everywhere. I imagined all of us connected like points of light in a constellation, fanning out until the world itself was held in a radiant net of love. Then I opened my eyes and gazed out at the sea, intensely aware that I was closer to the paths that the apostle Paul had walked than I ever might be again in my life. I found myself whispering, "Thank you, God. Thank you," over and over again like a mantra.

I pulled the Bible out of my pocket and read each account of the resurrection in the Gospels: Matthew 28, Mark 16, Luke 24, John 20. Then I took the vanilla wafer and the orange soda, lifted them up, gave thanks, and said, "Lord, I do this in remembrance of you." After receiving the elements, I sat for some time, feeling a deep connection to the Divine, to the mystery of Christ, and to all living things. Then, like some ancient version of church chimes, I began to hear in the distance the clinking and clunking of bells—cowbells, I thought, but that was the Ohioan in me. As they neared, the clinks were accompanied by the soft bleats of what I recognized as goats coming down the path. The sound was sweet and gentle, a perfect postlude to my Easter service.

I could hear the dull patter of their footsteps now and the occasional whistle and call of the goatherd, and I wondered for a moment what he might think if he caught a glimpse of me in the brush. Maybe I looked like a lost kid stuck in the brambles. Before I could think this through, a small face appeared. The first one down the path was the youngest of the herd. She must have sensed me there because she stopped suddenly and turned her head, eyeing me with curiosity. Not wanting to scare her, I didn't move a muscle. Then, to my surprise, the little goat leapt through the brush and onto a rock within reach of where I was sitting. We smiled at each other for a moment before I decided to take a chance and extend my arm. Like one accepting a customary greeting, the goat leaned in just close enough for me to scratch her nose with my finger. The moment was exquisite.

The bells were getting closer and the rest of the herd was almost in view when the little one turned and leapt back onto the path. The goatherd did, in fact, notice me sitting there as he passed by with his walking stick. He gave me a quizzical smile and a nod but did not break his stride. I lingered in the fading sound of hoofs and bleats, in the wonder of the gifts I had been given that morning, and in the wordless peace that passed from kid to kid.

"And that was probably one of the deepest spiritual experiences I have ever had," I concluded.

The dean's pause, though brief, was shockingly icy. "What you did was absolutely wrong," he said, barely able to contain his disdain, "on so many levels."

"What?"

"First of all," he continued, "you cannot give yourself communion. Only an ordained clergy*man* [my emphasis] can serve communion. Secondly, do you think an orange, much less orange soda, can turn into the blood of Christ?" His face was turning red and his voice was rising. "Only the juice of the grape can be used."

"Why?" I asked. I sat up a little straighter and squared my shoulders. "Jesus took what was at hand, which happened to be wine and unleavened bread, probably two of the most common things at the Jewish Passover table. Wasn't he telling them to remember him at all times, in every gathering, and in everything that nurtures the body and soul?" My heart was starting to pound and my eyes were narrowing. I only hoped that they wouldn't start spilling tears. I didn't want to give him the satisfaction of making me cry.

"Only the juice of the grape can be used because it alone turns into Christ's blood when you consume it. That's called transubstantiation."

Now I was not only hurt, I was mad, which was a good thing. It wasn't his theology that bothered me so much as his overbearing manner, his insensitivity and unfriendliness. Instead of inviting a conversation or an exchange of ideas, he chose to grind his heel into my spiritual back and denigrate the experience I had just shared with him. Without knowing what else to do, I lashed back. "That is the most arrogant thing I have ever heard. Does everyone have to think like you? I am a United Methodist and our communion juice does not, I assure you, turn into blood. Some of us see power in metaphor." I didn't wait for him to respond. Instead, I stood up and glanced at Chris, who looked pained and nervous. "Good luck here at Denison," I told him. I walked out of his office without saying another word, vaguely aware that Chris was right behind me; then the tears started to fall.

No wonder, thirty years later, the girl on the train with the kid at her side touched me so. The fragrance of orange, the extended hand, the rays of light through the sea of people, the sitting, the silence, the offering so meticulously prepared—all of these said *yes*, Christ is in the blood, but it is the blood that pumps between hearts. The spirit of Christ is just as present in the juice of a well-peeled orange as it is in the chalice on the altar. It is in the everyday things that we can remember him and remember who we are: namely, one herd with one shepherd, tripping along the path.

My Father's Eyes

I wasn't consciously aware that it was Father's Day as I slowly surfaced from sleep in the early hours of the morning. My cat, Julian, was mewing indignantly, demanding his breakfast regardless of the fact that it was only 5:30 a.m. on a Sunday. I pulled the covers over my head in an attempt to sink back into sleep and found myself resting in the resonance of a dream. Aware that it might soon escape me, I tried to soak in the details that were, at that moment, both vivid and fleeting.

In the dream, I went into the bathroom to wash my face. When I glanced in the mirror I saw my father standing behind me, smiling. He had been gone over two years but suddenly he was right there. "Dad!" I exclaimed, spinning around to face him. When I did, however, he had vanished. The space was empty, despite the very real image that I had just seen. Turning to face the mirror, I again saw him standing right behind me. He radiated vitality and love. I spun my head to look over my shoulder, torn between losing his image in the mirror and missing the sight of him behind me. But, again, he was not there. Once more I faced the mirror, this time confident that he would be standing behind me in the reflection. Sure enough, he was. We stood there, smiling as if this had been a silly game of hide-and-seek or a magic trick. Although I longed to turn around, I understood that I would not be able to see him if I did, and I wanted to hold on to this moment for as long as possible.

"Dad," I said, excitedly. "Dad . . . you're here!"

"Yes," he replied, nodding. "I'm here."

"I want to hug you!" I blurted.

"I know," he said gently. "But you can feel my hug, can't you?"

"Yes. Yes, I can."

I stood there for a few moments, looking into his eyes, feeling the warmth of his presence, and, more than that, his shimmering joy. On some level, I understood that I was seeing not only the person I knew as my father while he was alive, but also something closer to his essential, eternal spirit. It was as if the energy once contained in his body, with all its physical, emotional, and spiritual limitations, was now released. What I was experiencing was the pure essence of him, the spark of divinity that had resided in that dear, familiar frame. It washed over me and filled me with such happiness. And in that moment, any sorrow over his death evaporated, like a shadow completely consumed by sunlight.

I told him that I missed him here, in this life, although this wasn't said in a plaintive way. I wasn't asking him to come back. It was more like an affirmation, just another way of telling him that I loved him. He smiled knowingly and then he said, "You will never find me by looking backwards, but you will see me when you look in the mirror. My reflection is in you." I knew that he was teaching me many things at once—that he was speaking on levels that were both mysterious and tender. As I stood there, I felt like he was continuing to transfer lessons and wisdom without words. By remaining still, I could receive these, like a rock soaking in the warmth of the sun.

That's where I was when Julian's meows woke me. As my awareness shifted toward the sound, the mirror, along with Dad's image, disappeared like a mirage. I tried to reconstitute the images in my mind, but it was no longer a live feed. I was just back in my bed, replaying what I had experienced. Still, the feeling of being visited by my dad remained quite strong, as did his message: if I wanted to feel close to him, if I wanted to feel his presence, I would have to find him in myself and in the ways in which I see the world.

I always thought of my father as a magical person. If you told him a story or shared something that happened to you, he would find a thread of mystery and meaning in it. Dad interpreted everything that happened to him in a spiritual way. That's just the lens through which he viewed the world. Whether telling us a story about finding the star in the center of an apple or wondering whether the child he had seen was actually an angel, Dad's spiritual curiosity colored our days. Everything was a clue to the Holy: angels were waving their arms right in front of us, our deceased loved ones were there to guide us, and the "other side" was but one small step away. If the lights flickered as we spoke of someone who had died, Dad would try to intuit the message that was being communicated from the Beyond. If you told him of an encounter with a kind stranger, he would want to know all the details, helping you see how God might be working in your life. And if he held your hand to pray, you could feel the healing energy emanating from his palm. The depth and strength of his faith allowed him to be open to new insights, new avenues for experiencing the Divine.

I sometimes wonder if I have succeeded in giving this same gift to my children, if I have embodied, as he did, the delight in and the enthusiasm for mystery. I hope I have. It's part, after all, of their inheritance—not a financial inheritance but a spiritual one. We forget sometimes that we leave more than money or things to our loved ones. We leave a spiritual and moral legacy. The legacy my father left is rich. It is a jeweled tapestry of generosity, compassion, mysticism, and faith. If I fail to pass that gift on, then I have squandered something precious and irreplaceable. Then I will have truly lost him.

Sometime after the dream I had on Father's Day, I was mindlessly playing with an app on my cell phone called Snapchat. One of the silly possibilities of this app is to "face swap" with another person. And so, out of curiosity, I took a picture of myself and then found one of my dad. Using the app, our faces were not really *swapped*; more accurately, they were *blended*. The result took me by surprise. There he was, looking out of my eyes, and there was I, looking out of his. Either way, our images had merged. Even though he looked better in a beard than I did, I could literally see him in me. In our blended image, I could feel his warmth and his gentle spirit. And I experienced, in a deeper way, how much he loves me and how much of him still lives in me.

I often think of my mom, sitting in her kitchen, feeling the absence of my father every day. Where he went, she cannot yet follow. It's hard not to feel left behind when the one you love is no longer here. I would like to think that my dad *is* in fact both with her and beyond her. Just because she cannot see him doesn't mean he is not there. Maybe life is like a shell game. It's not that our loved ones are gone; we simply lose track of them. Our eyes cannot follow the hands that move them around. Perhaps they are simply hidden from our sight.

My father had a glimmer of this feeling once, many years ago, but it had a humorous conclusion. One day, he and Mom went to the grocery store. As he went down one aisle to get something, she continued on with the cart. After he got what he needed, he walked to the next aisle, looking for her. Then he walked to the next . . . and then the next . . . and then the next. Then he started to panic. She was nowhere in sight. *Where could she be?* he wondered. His heart raced with each empty aisle he passed. Some people might have gotten annoyed; some might have worried something terrible had happened to their partner. But not my father. Because of how he saw the world, his natural conclusion was *It's the rapture! And I've been left behind!*

Later, when he told the family this story, we all found it hilariously funny. Of course it was not the rapture, but rather one of those quirks of comic timing. He kept just missing her. As he had walked down one aisle, she had been on the next one. When he at last found her, he was enormously relieved. She, on the other hand, had been blissfully unaware of his absence and hadn't been worried about him at all. But the way he described it, it seemed entirely plausible that Mom could have been "taken up." And that possibility was both fascinating and riveting. He let it hang there in the air as we pictured our mother being lifted in a beam of light. The only thing that didn't stack up for us was the unlikely possibility that God would leave him here while the rest of the faithful were being collected for eternity.

It's terrifying to stand on the precipice of alone. We want our loved ones with us always. We often say to the bereaved after a loved one has died: he'll always be with you; she'll always be with you. While I believe this is true, it is difficult to grasp. What does it mean? That our loved ones are hanging out here on Earth until we join them? Somehow, I hope the veil between this world and the next is more permeable than that; that they are not stuck here but can move about freely, drawing near when we need them. Maybe it means that a part of them lives on in us and in our memories, that we can conjure them to the table with our laughter and can feel them beside us as we remember. And if we can feel our loved ones, even in their absence, if we can see them in ourselves, how much more should we aspire to feel and to see God in each other?

Several months after my dream, I was riding the subway in Manhattan. Glancing around at my fellow passengers, I made a mental note of how diverse the city is and marveled at how many different kinds of people and cultures can be represented in one subway car. One could say that I was consciously delighting in the gift of diversity. Then something strange began to happen. As I looked, each person's face began to transform right in front of me. The old Chinese woman with the weathered skin, the Latino man whose nose had surely been broken a time or two, the stunning young black woman with the elegant neck, the white kid with the buck teeth sitting across from me—all of them began to look . . . beautiful. It was like watching a moving montage with shifting colors and patterns. The more I stared, the more each part of every face became a wonder. I could not take my eyes off an ear or the waves on the bridge of a nose. I was in awe over the imperfect symmetry of someone's eyes. *Wow*, I thought. *Everyone is beautiful. We are all beautifully made.* I glanced around, curious if anyone else seemed to be seeing what I was seeing. If they did, they weren't saying.

In thinking about the experience, I believe two things happened. My vision became something closer to God's vision—I began to see the people on the train through God's eyes (and God sees us as inherently beautiful)—and I also saw God looking out at me through the eyes of these others. It's like we all did a face swap with God. Everyone's face was blended with God's face. It was a profound experience, one that I will never forget. In subsequent rides on the subway, I've tried to invoke the experience again by opening myself to see as God sees, but nothing has ever matched what happened spontaneously that day. One day, I told my daughter about it as we were boarding the train. "Can you see how beautiful everyone is?" I asked. "Yes, I think so!" she answered, smiling. And we rode like that, taking in beauty, until we reached our stop.

When I want to feel close to my dad, I try to look at the world through his eyes. How does he see it now in spirit form? I can feel him with me most strongly when I recognize beauty and I act with kindness and love, and I am grateful for the spiritual legacy he left. He taught me that the spirit of God is like a flame within each one of us. The more we offer love to one another, the more oxygen there is to feed the flame. Love is spiritual oxygen. Whether it's looking at the face swap with my dad or looking at the faces of strangers on a train, I know for certain that the indwelling Spirit in me is the same as the one in you. The indwelling Spirit in you is the same one in me. When we see as God sees, we are all beautiful and we are never alone.

Mysterium Tremendum et Fascinans

No, I have not just cast a spell from the Harry Potter books. The phrase *mysterium tremendum et fascinans* means "fearful and fascinating mystery." It is how the German theologian Rudolf Otto described having an encounter with the Holy; he called it a numinous experience. I first read his book *The Idea of the Holy* when I was a freshman in college. My theology professor, Dr. Walter Eisenbeis, challenged the class to go beyond childhood conceptions of God, of religion, and of spiritual experience, and venture into deeper waters, both academically and personally. It was a difficult but exciting class.

Having a genuine encounter with God is no small matter. It can be comforting, terrifying, or life changing; it may require something that we are afraid to do or to be. People like Moses and Job, Sarah and Mary knew this, but most of us can't believe these kinds of encounters happen today. Perhaps we are numb to mystery—or maybe a part of us is truly afraid for what might follow if God spoke to us. It's not what we know but what we do *not* know and cannot understand when it comes to the Divine. *Mysterium tremendum et fascinans* is Otto's way of capturing this feeling. And in our modern, day-to-day life, when little astounds us, it's important to keep in mind the possibility of encountering the "wholly other," in the face of which we can only be silent.

If we have the courage to entertain the possibility that the Holy is not confined to our limited conceptions, to what we can tolerate or understand, then we might find ourselves on a new path, personally and spiritually. And this is where the adventure begins. A mystical encounter with God is not limited to that which is inspired by a sunset or by pondering the starry expanse, by the miracle of birth or by Nature, even when she occasionally shakes her hurricane fist at us. What Otto and others describe is more like the trembling terror of standing before a burning bush and removing one's shoes. That gesture of humility is really all we've got.

Things we don't understand often make us uncomfortable. This is especially true when it comes to spiritual experiences. While listening to someone tell a story about a goose-bumpy moment or a feeling of being in the presence of the "wholly other," we *want* to believe it but often are filled with doubt. We are like Thomas listening to the rest of the disciples as they talked about seeing Jesus after he died. He must've been kicking himself. Maybe he'd drawn the short straw and had to make a food run. Maybe he was the only one brave enough to step out of the room and find out what was happening in town. Either way, he had to have been listening with a mixture of astonishment and envy, his heart burning to believe them but his rational mind unable to accept it. Theirs was a numinous experience of unparalleled power. And when one has had such an experience, words like "amazing," "astonishing," "fascinating," "miraculous," and "supernatural" are used in an attempt to explain it. What's crucial to note is that, as one writer puts it, "The numinous is not a projection of something inside the personality; it comes from a radically different beyond."[2]

The idea of a "radically different beyond" is at the heart of religious experience and mystical pondering. We cannot prove there is something

---

2   Jesse Thomas, "From Joy to Joy: C.S. Lewis and the Numinous in the World of Relationships", 1998.

beyond this life, but we can contemplate it, we can aspire to it—and some claim to have glimpsed it. Contemplating mystery means being open to the intersection of two worlds: the one we live in and the one that might exist beyond our gaze.

My parents were spiritual explorers, a regular Lewis and Clark team leading the family on an expedition to the Unknown. They were open to the mystical, while at the same time deeply rooted in their Christian faith. Any moments when we sensed we were not alone, when our hearts started to pound and our mouths went dry, were shared around the kitchen table with enthusiasm and interest. It was fun. We were on to something. We were all part of the discovery team, and any one of us had the ability to find a clue to what waited beyond the curtain. The world was saturated with mystery and all mystery pointed to the existence of God.

So when my dad began to tell us about the visitor who had knocked on the door one night when we were little, we knew it might involve the possibility of an encounter with an angel—or what I would now consider a numinous experience. "It was a snowy December evening," he began. "All of you children were tucked in for the night, and Mom and I finally had a moment to relax. Suddenly, we heard a knock on the door."

With that, we were captivated. When Dad was in story mode, especially a story involving spiritual phenomena, nothing could distract us. He went on to explain how he and my mom were startled by the knock. It was unusual for anyone to knock at that hour unless it was an emergency. We lived on a small cul-de-sac with modest houses, inhabited mostly by young families. The houses stood shoulder to shoulder. In the summer, voices could be heard through the open windows, but in winter, we were zipped up as snugly as a wool sweater.

Dad opened the door, hoping it wasn't some kind of emergency. Standing there in the gently falling snow was not a neighbor with a problem or a favor to ask, but a man in a short-sleeved button-down shirt. Just beyond him, the neighbors' little houses glowed with Christmas lights, Charlie Brown–style—imperfect, humble, sweet. The man explained that he was collecting money for some kind of charity and that any donation would be appreciated. Dad paused before answering, conscious of the fact that it was a curious moment and a curious stranger, and that he had five children sleeping inside. "Wait here," he said, "and let me see if I have any cash to give you." We never had extra money in those early years, especially just before Christmas; in fact, money was tight. But my father never refused to give when asked, so he rifled through his pockets and came back with a few dollars. "Thank you," said the man when my father handed him the bills. "God bless you."

With that, the stranger turned to leave and Dad went back inside. Thinking about the curious interaction, he returned to his chair but when he tried to sit down, he later explained, he could not. "It was like an invisible force was keeping me from sitting," he told us, his face animated. "I kept trying to sit down but something wouldn't let me." As he spoke, Dad got up from his place at the kitchen table and showed us how he had tried to sit but was blocked by some unseen force field. We were on the edge of our seats now, on the edge of something magical and mysterious. *What happened next?* we wanted to know. *What did you do?*

"When I couldn't sit," he explained, "I ran back to the door and the man was still standing there. 'Hold on!' I told him. 'I have something else for you.'" Dad described again the man's short-sleeved shirt and the falling snow. He knew he had more to give.

"And so I ran to the closet and pulled out my suit," he said.

"Your *only* suit," reminded my mother, shaking her head and laughing.

"Yes, my only suit; the one I need to go to work in."

He had picked it up from the dry cleaner earlier in the day and it was still in its clear plastic wrapping. "Here," he said, thrusting the suit toward the man, "I think this should fit you." Without asking any questions, the man took the suit, hanger and all, a small smile lighting his face. "God bless you," he said again quietly. "Merry Christmas."

"I went back inside," Dad said, "and this time I was able to sit. But then I thought, how stupid! I should have given him something warm, like my winter coat." He described grabbing his coat and running back to the front door. But not only was the man gone, there were no footprints to follow in the snow. Coat in hand, Dad ran next door and asked if anyone strange had knocked on their door. "Just you," the neighbors laughed. "Just you." Undaunted, he continued around the cul-de-sac, inquiring the same thing of each neighbor but receiving the same baffled look, the same answer.

"I stood for a moment looking back at our house," he said. "It was so quiet. The snow was falling silently and light glowed from our windows. Then I heard these words from scripture: 'Do not neglect to show hospitality to strangers, for thereby some have entertained angels unawares.'"[3]

"So you think that man was an angel, Dad?" we asked, our eyes wide.

"Maybe," he answered with a smile. "That's the only explanation I can come up with."

"But what did you do about going to work without your suit?"

"God took care of me," he said, smiling that mysterious smile. And he went on to explain how a cousin's husband had died very suddenly a day or two later, a man who was the same size as he was, a man who happened to have two suits hanging in his closet that he would no longer need. "I gave one suit away and got two in return," he said.

It's not just the story of the Christmas visitor that I remember, it's the way my father told it, the way he saw meaning in it, and the multitextured message it conveyed. He wanted to teach us about kindness

---

3   Hebrews 13:2, English Standard Version.

and compassion, about giving, even when you don't have much to give, about choosing faith over fear and recognizing mystery when it knocks on your door. My parents softened our spirits like clay so that we could feel the impressions left by the brush of angel wings. They taught us to notice the ripples on the surface of our spiritual waters and to contemplate the nature of the invisible breeze. They taught us to open our hearts to the presence of God, trusting that God's heart is always open to us.

I was reminded of this not long ago, when I came upon an elderly man weeping at the grave of his wife in a large cemetery in the Bronx. I had just finished officiating the funeral of a stranger, something that I am asked to do on numerous occasions in my role as a minister. When it was over and the family had departed, I took a moment to walk the grounds. I was in Woodlawn Cemetery, a historical landmark and one of the largest cemeteries in New York City. I was aware that many notable people were buried in these grounds, including the musicians Irving Berlin, George M. Cohan, Miles Davis and Duke Ellington, and author Herman Melville, just to name a few. It was a lovely fall day, the kind of day where as many leaves still cling to the branches as crunch underfoot. The bright blue sky and the fiery leaves seemed even more brilliant when set against the white of the headstones and monuments. I knew I'd have little chance of stumbling upon one of the musicians' graves, even with a map, but thought I'd stroll around. At four hundred acres and over three hundred thousand graves, Woodlawn conceals its dead very well. If one was looking to get lost, this just might be the place.

I was taking my time as I walked along, half looking at the headstones and half looking at the blue sky, when I saw the elderly gentleman. He was standing alone, gazing down at a grave, one that was tucked off to the side of the path and obscured by some tall, scruffy shrubs. The shrubs had mostly shed their leaves, which were scattered carelessly here and there in little piles, like remnants from a party, leaving their spindly branches exposed. I suppose that's partly why I saw him there—the bare branches waved me over with a thousand black-gloved hands. Although I could tell that he was crying, because he would occasionally wipe his eyes with a handkerchief, I wasn't sure whether I should intrude on his solitude.

I stood there for a moment, aware that if I took a step, the crunching of the leaves beneath my feet would give me away. It was a painfully beautiful picture. Leaves were gently floating to the ground, trees were reaching for the sky, and this man was standing somewhere between heaven and earth. I took a few steps, intentionally brushing away some leaves underfoot to announce my presence. I didn't want to startle him, nor was I intent on engaging him. I thought we would exchange a polite smile and I would move on. But when the man looked up, his face was a mixture of wonder and joy. It was not what I expected at all.

"Excuse me," he said, his eyes wide, tears still spilling. "Did you pass a young man walking around just now?" No, I told him, I had not. I asked if he was waiting for someone, thinking a family member was perhaps supposed to come back for him.

"Do you need a ride?" I asked him. "Can I help you find him?"

"Oh no," he said, shaking his head. "It's just that . . . well . . . the strangest thing just happened."

He went on to tell me about how he had come to the cemetery to visit his wife's grave. Although he didn't come every day, he came almost every week to place flowers or to clear the brush off her stone. For some reason, whether he had parked in a different place or had lost his bearings in the shifting fall landscape, he could not find her grave. "I was getting more and more upset," he told me. The more upset he became, the less sure he was about which way to walk. Finally, he said, he just stopped walking and broke down in tears.

"I didn't know what else to do," he said, searching my face. "I just stood there and cried. And I guess I prayed. Then the most amazing thing happened. This young man approached me and asked if I was

OK. I explained to him that I had gotten lost and that I couldn't find where my wife was buried. Can you imagine that," he asked, shaking his head, "not being able to find your beloved's grave?"

I was starting to get chills, the way you do when you know something unexplainable is going to be revealed. "What happened?" I asked gently, feeling like a child listening to one of my dad's stories again.

"He asked me what her name was. Now, don't get me wrong. I thought that was nice but pretty pointless. Look around at this place. It's huge. But I told him anyway, and when I did, he said, 'Oh, I know exactly where she is. Follow me.'"

The gentleman gestured in the direction of where he was when he had gotten lost and had stopped walking, which was nowhere near where we were standing. "It's not like I was three feet away," he continued. But the stranger walking beside him led him, without hesitation, to the place where his wife was buried.

"I was so overcome with emotion when we got to her spot," he said, "that I just burst into tears again. And when I looked up to thank him, he was gone."

After letting those words sink in for a moment, he smiled. "You probably think I'm crazy, don't you? A crazy old man."

"No, I don't," I told him. "I think God sent you an angel."

We stood together for a few more minutes, gazing at his wife's grave and sharing the wonder of what had just happened. He scratched his head and tried to impress upon me the unlikelihood of a stranger, especially a stranger whom he had never seen, knowing where his wife was buried. After coming week after week for a year, he explained, he was at least visually familiar with many of those who visited nearby graves, but he had never seen this man. Our words floated in the air like the gently falling leaves until I sensed him drifting into a more private place. We gave each other a warm hug, then I asked him if he could find his way out. With a little chuckle, he answered, yes, he sure could. Then, looking down at his wife's gravestone, he said, "Hey, by the way . . . it's our anniversary today."

Sometimes the Holy materializes when we are most in need, in ways and in forms that we can recognize and understand; other times, we must go on faith. Whether we choose to see the things that happen in our lives as coincidence, serendipity, luck, or divine intervention is up to us. Whether human or divine, the stranger who appeared to guide the grieving man was the incarnation of an answered prayer. It doesn't matter to me—and I don't want to know—if he was a groundskeeper, a regular visitor to the cemetery, or an apparition. The moment was holy. The more open we are, the more we will experience the numinous, and the more we will whisper, *mysterium tremendum et fascinans.*

The Sacred Pause

Most of us need reminding that we are loved—by one another and by God. Without this awareness, life is inherently lonely. I tell my children every day, multiple times a day, that I love them. I can aspire to embody this love by accepting and celebrating the totality of who they are, by showing up for their events, and by being present for them. The love they inspire in me, and the love that they return, is a circular flow, like a continually refreshing spring. If their spirits should sag, I hope that they will have moments and images that refill their wells.

One image that I treasure happened after a hard-won and emotional win at my son's college football game. Standing in the end zone after the game, I could see him making his way off the field from thirty yards out. His helmet was off, and he was walking with the determined stride of someone on a mission. Teammates were patting his shoulder pads as he passed; parents stopped to say congratulations. Alex smiled and nodded, but he kept moving through the crowd. Then we locked eyes. When he reached me, my six-foot-three, 200-pound son grabbed me in a sweaty embrace, his head on my shoulder, wet cheek pressed against mine, and he was overcome with emotion. "Thanks for being here, Mom," he said, his voice shaking. "Thanks for coming to every game. I love you so much."

I wanted to hold on to that moment, not only for myself, but for him. Because I *was* there, he *could* feel my love in a physical, tangible way, and one day, when he needs it, he might remember. I knew that it was more than an emotional win that prompted the outpouring from my son. He was conscious of the fact that I had almost died during surgery the year before and that there had been a real possibility that I'd never attend another game—and he was overwhelmed by gratitude and love. If I had brushed it off as just the end to another football game, I would have missed the blessing inherent in my son's grateful embrace.

Mothering is a divine activity—whether we have given birth to our children or have adopted them, whether we are men or women— because mothering (in a larger sense) means helping to bring another person into full being. It means agreeing to be home base for another, being the mother ship. It means providing a safe, nurturing space where another can feel wholly cherished and loved. Meister Eckhart said, "We are all meant to be mothers of God. God is always needing to be born." We give birth to God every moment that we usher love into the world.

Ushering love into the world can take many forms. Sometimes it means gently ushering someone out of this world and into the next. Such was the case of a young nurse I encountered many years ago. I was giving a lecture at a nursing school to a group of soon-to-be graduating nurses. While discussing spirituality and end of life, I asked if any of the students had been with a patient who was dying. A young nurse raised her hand. She quietly described how she'd arrived at the hospital one evening for her shift. It was a busy time. The regular staff nurses were preparing for the shift change by triaging and reporting on their patients. As the student made her way toward the nursing station, something—or rather, someone—caught her eye. Through the open door of one of the patient rooms, she noticed an elderly woman who had become uncomfortably twisted in the bed.

Not wanting to report late for her shift, the young nurse hesitated before deciding to enter the room. Once inside, she gently straightened the patient into a more comfortable position, adjusted her pillow, and smoothed her covers. It was then that she realized the patient appeared to be dying. In a moment of panic, she was unsure what to do. Should she run down the hall to get a seasoned nurse, or at least call out for help? Choosing to stay with the woman, the nurse took her hand. When she did, the patient looked into the eyes of the young student nurse, whispered "Thank you," and breathed her last breath.

Tears streamed down the student's cheeks as she told the story. "I didn't know what to do," she explained. "But I couldn't bear to leave her."

I hope that I was able to help her see that she had stepped into God's scrubs for a moment, that her loving-kindness was a gift to the dying woman, and that the woman repaid that gift of kindness with gratitude. At a glance, it might have looked like a scene that plays out every day in countless hospitals around the world. People die, nurses and doctors do their best, life goes on. But God is in the pause; holiness is in the hidden places of the heart. The nurse ushered love into the world at the moment she paused and turned toward another's suffering, and the dying woman ushered in love when she acknowledged this gesture with gratitude, even in the midst of her suffering. In the intimacy of that moment, they were mothering each other into and with the arms of God.

God on the Corner

The snow was falling heavily as my friend Andrea and I walked arm in arm along the busy shopping district in Vienna. It was as if an invisible hand had shaken a giant snow globe in which we were but tiny figures. Squeezing past us on the sidewalks were elegant women in fur coats, men in hats with feathers, and children bundled in forest-green wool. The distinct clip of Viennese-accented German floated in the crisp, muted air. Some words and phrases were already beginning to sound recognizable to me, though most slipped by like snippets of a song I couldn't quite make out. But for the slap of winter on my cheeks and the slight stinging in my toes, I might have been moving through a dream.

I had come to Vienna for a semester abroad during my junior year of college. Like many students, I wanted to take advantage of the opportunity to travel, to experience living in another country, and to be immersed in a foreign language. At first, I wasn't sure how I could afford to do this, but I soon learned that all of my financial aid would transfer to the international program. All I needed was a loan for my airfare, a borrowed backpack, and a little courage.

Two days after landing in Vienna, I was introduced to Andrea, who became my new roommate. She grew up on Long Island and was a junior at Ithaca College. Although we had very little in common except the desire to become fluent in German and to fully live this experience, our bond was immediate. Ironically, we were both "Andreas," although I went by Andie. Her parents were nonreligious Jews; mine were religious Methodists. Her mother was a pediatrician whose parents escaped Nazi Germany in the '30s, eventually settling in Argentina. Her father, a psychiatrist, was a Hungarian Jew who spent five years of his childhood in a concentration camp. Most of his family and friends were murdered during the Holocaust.

My mother, on the other hand, grew up on a farm in Kentucky. She managed a pediatrician's office for twenty-five years but could have run a large corporation. My father, a writer, was born and raised in a German neighborhood of Cincinnati. Countless members of his community, including his uncle, went off to fight the Nazis, many of them knowing that they would be fighting against relatives.

In those ways, Andrea and I could not have been more different. Maybe that's why our personalities and backgrounds seemed to fit together like puzzle pieces. She had a wonderful irreverence that made me laugh and prompted me to look at the world from a different angle. She could swear like a sailor, something she tried to teach me to do with impressive creativity, but my upbringing inhibited me from truly mastering it. I was fascinated by her accent (New York was like a foreign country to me), by her family history, her passion, and her warmth. We used to joke that I knew more about Judaism than she did because her family was not observant. Andrea was fiery, adventurous, and loyal; I was mellow, maybe a little too trusting, but always open to a new experience. Though I was often short on cash, she never made me feel bad about it, even when it hindered our ability to go out together, and I never minded if she did things without me. Such was the ease of our friendship.

Our plan as we strolled together was to settle in at one of Vienna's famous cafés, warm up with a cup of something delicious, practice our German, and plan our next adventure. What we were talking about as we walked, I can't recall, but I'm sure we were laughing. I can still sense the lightness of our spirits, can still feel the rhythm of our synchronized steps and the padded bump of our shoulders as we walked along arm in arm. And I remember the moment that everything changed. It was like stumbling on a tripwire.

Standing still as a statue, as if frozen in place, was an elderly man with a long beard and a tin cup in his hand. He wore a tattered coat and no gloves. His head was bowed and his countenance was one of utter humility. We immediately fell silent as we passed him, both of us aware, on some level, that we had been shattered. Not shattered by grief or even compassion, really—that was not it. We were shattered by the pure humanity of him and by the incongruence of his presence there amid the bustle and flow, the commerce and the light-hearted chatter.

Andrea was no stranger to seeing people beg. She had grown up in and around New York City and was accustomed to the presence of pan-handlers and the homeless. She had learned how to steel herself, how to look straight ahead and to keep moving. While I was less worldly, I wasn't completely sheltered from the reality of poverty on the streets. But this man shook us. He shook us not because we had never seen someone asking for change, but because of something in his presence.

We walked a few blocks in silence, the mood between us suddenly somber and searching, then we began to share how we had never seen someone like him on the streets of Vienna . . . or anywhere for that matter. There was something profoundly moving about him, something we couldn't articulate but could feel, like when you know something true has been spoken or the arrow has hit its mark. Stopping abruptly in our tracks, we looked at each other and knew we had to go back. It was like heading the wrong way down a one-way street. People continued streaming past us on the sidewalk, bumping and nudging and appearing slightly annoyed at our deviation from the customary orderliness.

A sense of urgency and purpose descended as we ran back through the falling snow. We had no plan. A quick assessment of the contents of our pockets revealed that we had, between us, the equivalent of about three dollars, which we had planned to spend on our coffees. After a block or two, we passed a street vendor selling thick slices of salty potatoes that were roasted over a steel barrel and then scooped into paper cones. The smell of them could make your mouth water from half a block away. Maybe it was the aroma or maybe it was because we were hungry ourselves, but we made a spontaneous decision to buy the man some food. I handed over my one *schilling*, agreeing that whatever we had left should be given to the stranger.

We continued on, pushing our way through the bundled figures, some of whom lumbered along like circus bears. We strained to see through the thick curtain of white, hoping that the man was still there. Just where *there* was, we weren't entirely certain, but we kept moving in the general direction. *Please be there. Please be there,* I whispered as we squeezed past shoppers, past women with children, past elderly couples linked arm in arm. *Please be there.* The words escaped in little white puffs like incense from a censer.

As we rounded a corner, we saw him. I exhaled, finally, relief and gratitude melting the tension in my chest. He was standing motionless, just like before, with eyes downcast and head bowed. His stillness created a strange dissonance with the never-ending flow of time and humanity. It appeared as if he were invisible to the parade of people passing by, as if he weren't even there. No one slowed a step; no one turned a head, raised an eyebrow, or acknowledged him in any way. And yet, even from a distance, the vibration he emanated was palpable. He was like a distant star that had fallen to earth, but from whom light still fanned out across the frozen human tundra.

Coming closer, I noticed that his expression was neither sad nor broken: it was gentle. Because I didn't expect this, I found it strangely disarming. Snow collected in his beard and fell heavily on his soft gray hair. He wore no hat, he spoke no words—he simply offered his cup, like a prayer, while countless feet shuffled by without pause. We came to a stop directly in front of him, and I was suddenly aware that

Andrea and I hadn't contemplated what we were going to say if and when we found him again. At first, he didn't seem to notice us standing there—this time, it was *we* who were invisible—and a momentary silence descended.

"*Entschuldigen,*" I finally stammered. Excuse me. His eyes slowly lifted. They were gray, like his beard, but bright—and I felt the light pass right through me.

I'd seen eyes like that only once before: they belonged to a monk I had encountered at a monastery while on a college retreat with my Mysticism class. Although not a Catholic, I'd been given permission to receive communion. When the monk offered me the host, he looked into my eyes—and it felt like he could see down into the depths of me, like he knew all my shortcomings and secrets, my strengths and my flaws. The monk's eyes were like liquid silver, like lightning. Sparks seemed to fly from them, as if a cosmic flint were being struck against the inside of his skull. I felt suddenly shy and exposed. I wanted to look away. But as I continued looking into his eyes, I realized that I saw no judgment there. There was only love. And it scared me a little.

The eyes of the homeless man contained the same light, but they were softer around the edges. They burned like the fire of a hearth, familiar and inviting. As we held each other's gaze, warmth seeped into my body, filling my chest and spilling down my arms and legs. I felt like the Tin Man from *The Wizard of Oz*, oiled and released at last from my inertia. Not knowing what else to do, I extended the steaming potatoes to him.

"*Das ganze?*" he whispered. The whole thing? The lot? The all? I nodded. He bent down quickly to set his cup on the ground, then carefully took the paper cone in both of his hands. *Das ganze*, responded my heart. The All. The Universe in a paper cup. We had passed it as gently and as lovingly as a newborn. For a moment the three of us stood there smiling, like old friends who were sharing a cup of coffee or an inside joke, but in essence what we were sharing was communion. We were a tattered trinity, revealed, exposed, and yet unnoticed.

An eternity seemed to pass, although the exchange lasted mere seconds. I was vaguely aware of Andrea leaning down to drop her money into his cup, the lonely clink of her coins revealing that it had been empty. He gave a little bow, and there was an awkward pause. Instinctively, we knew that he wasn't going to eat with us staring at him, and so we waved good-bye and turned to go.

"Guess we'll have to bag the coffee," Andrea said dryly, "since we're broke now." I shrugged, she rolled her eyes—the call and response of our friendship grounding us again. Then we linked arms and let silence fall between us as we made our way home. But in that space was the gentle presence of the man we'd just encountered, and it accompanied us with a warm arm around our shoulders.

Over the next few weeks, I would occasionally trek back to the street where we had seen him. Each time, I would bring a little money, a hat or a scarf, a pair of gloves or some warm socks, but I never saw him again. Although I'm not sure why, I never told Andrea about these sojourns. I guess I was shy about sharing my impression that he was an angel. Maybe we only get one opportunity to touch holiness—or maybe we get many every moment of every day but miss what is right in front of us. Whatever the case, I will always be grateful for that second chance—the day we turned and found God still standing on the corner.

It's in the Stars

It was Friday night and the local high school football game was in its last quarter. I had stopped by to watch some of the game, even though my football-playing son was now a freshman in college. It was something that never got old—for me and for plenty of others in our small town. If you didn't have a son playing, you either knew someone who did, were an alumnus, or simply enjoyed sitting in the stands on a cool October evening to cheer on the home team. I felt a bit wistful next to my friend Dale, whose youngest son was still in high school. My son's years on that field had flown by all too quickly. Try as we might, no amount of savoring can slow the passage of time.

Dale and I made plans to meet after the game. Since I knew she would want to chat with her son and with the other players' moms, I decided to head home a little early and wait for her call. As I walked, I could hear the familiar voice of the announcer floating through the night air, growing fainter and more muffled with each step. There was something comforting about the sound, but it also made me nostalgic for the years when my children were small and, perhaps, for my own high school years in Ohio. When I was growing up, Friday nights in the fall meant football. They meant my mother's chili on the stove and quick changes from cheerleading uniforms into jeans. They meant bonfires and dates. They meant riding around with friends in my beat-up car, looking for a party, or hanging out in the parking lot of the local pizzeria until the cops shooed us on our way. Friday nights were iconic. And they continued to be so, even as I eventually morphed from the cheerleader on the field to the mom in the stands.

My mood was both relaxed and reflective as I waited at home for Dale's call. In the meantime, I opened my computer and did the usual noodling around, checking my e-mail and scanning the news. For some reason, I decided to visit Amazon and take a peek at how my second book, *Incognito: Lost and Found at Harvard Divinity School*, was doing. It had been out for six months. When it was first published, I would find myself occasionally scanning the book's Amazon page to see if there were any new reviews and to keep track of how it seemed to be doing. I was driven in equal parts by curiosity and excitement—and probably a little trepidation. *Incognito* recounted my time in divinity school, which included mixed-up relationships and various expressions of self-doubt, as well as my path toward the ministry. It was quite different in tone than my first book, *The Voice That Calls You Home.* At least that one, if not as humorous, bore the dignity, gravitas, and (hopefully) maturity of my later work as a hospice chaplain.

When I pulled up *Incognito* on Amazon, I didn't expect to see any great leap in the ranking, or even any new reviews, so I glanced at the screen with benign detachment. What I saw, however, made me sit bolt upright and lean into the computer. A new review had just been posted, punctuated with one lonely star. *Ouch.* But that wasn't the worst of it. The reviewer went on to say that she would have given the book *no* stars, if that were an option. *Huh.* I respect the fact that not everyone is going to love a book or find it helpful. There are better writers and better stories than mine. Still . . . in my most insecure moment, even *I* would give *Incognito* at least one humble star. Now I felt intrigued.

The reviewer explained how she was hoping to apply to divinity school herself and that the book wasn't helpful (I was sorry to hear that). Furthermore, she felt it could not possibly be true (she was wrong there). Among other things, she concluded that it read like an A+ college essay (well, at least I had that going for me).

I sat for some time blinking at the words on my computer screen, trying to take them in. What began to dawn was a growing curiosity about this particular reviewer. There was something in her words, something in the way that she hurled her fury, that made me want to reach out to her. I can't even tell you why. Although I was sorry that she hadn't found the book helpful, that's not what was driving me. It was what I heard between the lines—namely, the voice of someone who was searching for her path but wasn't sure how to get there.

I wanted to respond to her review, but I was a little embarrassed that I had even seen it in the first place. Responding to someone's comment was a first for me, and I didn't want to come off sounding creepy or defensive. And so I typed the only thing I could think of that came close to capturing my intentions: *Would love to have a conversation with you.* Then I signed my name and hit the comment button.

The next night, I checked Amazon to see if she had responded. She had. Clearly, she was surprised and rattled that I had read her review, and she was worried she may have hurt my feelings. I assured her that wasn't why I had written to her. Her response was so genuine. It affirmed my initial sense that this was a person with whom I would like to dialogue. In a spirit of friendship, I offered to send her *The Voice That Calls You Home*, thinking she might enjoy it more, and I encouraged her to keep in touch. The next day, however, when I checked to see if she had replied, her review had been deleted. I was truly sorry about that because it prevented any further exchange with her. The only thing I knew was her first name: Kitty.

Over the next couple of weeks, I checked periodically to see if Kitty had posted another comment, but I never found one. I thought of her often and was sad to think that she had disappeared before we had the chance to talk about divinity school. I wondered about her journey and hoped that she was finding support. Thinking of our brief exchange always made me smile, and I kept her in my prayers. Finally, it occurred to me to take a look at the reviews for *The Voice That Calls You Home*. And there it was: a review from Kitty.

She began by telling the story of how she came upon the book, which included her initial criticism of *Incognito* and our subsequent exchange. I laughed when she wrote that she was worried she had "done pissed off a priest," and my heart went out to her as she shared about feeling like a "jerk." Kitty, I knew, was anything but a jerk. Finally, after making some very moving remarks about *The Voice*, she concluded with this:

> And I can't believe I wrote those things about *Incognito*. Seriously I cannot sleep after reading this book, knowing she read my stupid review. I hope she can see this and know the comfort and guidance she has given me through this book of powerful essays. Thank you, if you're reading this; that is all I have to say.[4]

I replied to tell her how glad I was to have found her again, and thus began my friendship with Kitty. We continued our correspondence privately, via e-mail, rather than through the public forum of an Amazon review. Over the next few months, I would learn that she came to this country from China when she was thirteen years old, that the death of her grandmother had a profound impact on her search for meaning and faith, and that she already had a master's degree in creative writing. What's more, she was an incredible artist and had been a solo long-haul truck driver, professional translator, and screenwriter of Chinese feature films. In short, I learned that Kitty was an extraordinary young woman of depth and substance, intelligence and life experience; she blew me away. And so, just a couple months after our "accidental" meeting online, she asked me to take a look at her application essays for Harvard

---

4   For Kitty's complete review, go to www.amazon.com.

Divinity School. They were brilliant. More than a tweak from me, what she needed was affirmation of her own greatness. I was honored to give that to her.

Later that spring, I received a tag on Facebook that directed me to her page. There it was: the acceptance letter to Harvard Divinity School, along with a kind word addressed to me. In all honesty, Kitty would have gotten into Harvard quite easily without my two cents. She is incredibly smart. She is compassionate. She is forging her destiny with courage and faith. She feels called to be a hospice chaplain, especially ministering to the underserved Chinese population in Northern California. That's where her family settled when they arrived in this country; that's where her grandmother died. Her understanding of culture, language, and world religions, as well as her sensitivity, will make her an unbelievable chaplain, of this I am certain.

Kitty arrived at Harvard Divinity School about a year after reading *Incognito*, which takes place at the same school almost thirty years earlier. In some ways, it's no wonder it seemed unreal to her! And at the same time, it's hard to imagine Harvard Divinity until you experience it. Kitty and I had kept in touch through the summer via e-mail, and I couldn't wait for her to begin what I knew would be an incredible few years. We made plans to meet in person once she got settled. When that time came, I drove from New York to Cambridge, contemplating the unlikely circumstances that brought us together. It was dark and was pouring rain when I neared her apartment. Leaning forward in my seat, I strained to read the street numbers through the motion of the wipers and the rain hitting my windshield. Then I saw her—a petite, hooded figure standing on the street holding an umbrella. Concerned that I might miss her driveway, she had been watching for me. I parked and we gave each other a quick, nervous hug before running inside her apartment to get out of the rain.

Once inside, I couldn't stop smiling. Her tiny room in the shared apartment reminded me of my own during my first year, and I immediately loved Kitty's presence, which was both shy and powerful. We went across the street to grab a bite and began to take each other in . . . to take in the mystery of how we met and the genuine bond we had formed. *This is what can happen when we take time to read between the lines,* I thought. *This is what happens when we let the Spirit nudge us.*

Speaking of nudges from the Spirit . . . I hadn't intended to tell this story about Kitty, but then I got a pretty clear sign. I was driving back home to New York from Ohio, where I had spent the weekend watching my son play college football. My "spirit daughter" Sorcha, a teenager to whom I had become close after her mother had died, was with me. We were talking about the strange circumstances that often draw people together, as they had she and I, and I began telling her about Kitty. After describing how we had crossed paths in a funny exchange online, I mentioned how Kitty had driven a truck, an eighteen-wheeler, which (to me) said a lot about her courage, her strength, and her adventurous spirit. At that moment, a huge truck pulled up alongside of us. I started to point out to Sorcha that this was the size of truck Kitty had driven, not just a small pickup but one made for heavy, long-haul trucking. Then I stopped midsentence. As the truck passed us, I saw that its bright orange cab had the unmistakable Schneider logo printed in large letters on its side. "Actually," I laughed. "That's not only the *kind* of truck Kitty drove, that's the company she drove for." I guess I need billboard-size (or at least truck-size) signs from God when it comes to certain things.

If Kitty ever decides to write about her experiences at Harvard Divinity School, I hope I am around to read them. Clearly, her words will be different from mine. They will be colored by her unique life, her views, her struggles, and the soaring achievements that are sure to come. But I hope that wonder will also rise from the pages like the ripples of heat from pavement. I hope there will be laughter, captured in a cup of truck-stop coffee. And maybe there will even be the equivalent of a Friday night spent waiting for a friend and finding, instead, a fellow hitchhiker on the journey.

Saints of Light

Every year, as August rolls to a lazy stop and summer vacations give way to school shopping, I'm distracted by the persistent and weighty reality that September 11 is coming around again. After so many years of anticipating this anniversary, I shouldn't be surprised by my feelings, but I always am. It's like falling for the same trick over and over again, or like knowing where the rake in the grass is but stepping on it anyway, then being shocked by the inevitable whack in the face. The first days of September are like that for me. They form an unavoidable gauntlet. Despite my efforts to brace myself, I have yet to find an effective way in which to prepare for the sucker punch that is guaranteed to land on 9/11. I tell myself that time has passed, that I helped as much as I could at Ground Zero, that I would volunteer all over again if called. I picture families who lost their loved ones, and workers who showed up day after day to search for bodies, to move mountains of debris, to comfort the grieving, and I say a prayer. In short, I remember.

Still, September 11 has created a fissure, a fault line in my life; it marks a *before* and an *after*. Even as I write that, I am mindful of the luxury of *having* an after. My life did not end on 9/11, but it was frayed by the aftershocks. In some ways, the anniversary of that day allows me a chance to admit the pain and the sorrow that I carry from my experiences of working as a chaplain at the morgue on site. Most of the time, these feelings rest in the shadows. I know that they are there, but I do not often invite them to step into the light. I wouldn't know where to go with them, anyway. Unless one was directly affected by the attacks on 9/11, it's not something that most people are thinking about—not anymore. In the immediate aftermath of that day, and even on the first few anniversaries, September was, in essence, a river of tears. Individually and as a nation, we were drowning in them. After five years, the shock was starting to wear off, and the numbness that can accompany trauma was giving way to the excruciating permanence of loss. Our collective pain was still palpable, as was our defiant determination to remember, but we were beginning to move on (whatever that means). After ten years, we still honored the losses but, as a nation, we seemed to be returning the dead to their families. The grieving became more singular and private. What about in twenty years? Will the rituals we have created to give voice to the pain of that day become so routine that we no longer feel it? Perhaps this is understandable and unavoidable. But for those who are intimately connected by the loss of a loved one or by the experience of helping in some way, September 11 will always press its sharp point into a tender wound.

As a recent anniversary of that day approached, I found myself overwhelmed with sadness. Although the town in which I live had lost fifteen of its citizens, its memorial service had grown smaller and smaller. I knew, of course, that the families of those who died would be remembering and grieving, mostly privately, but I didn't know what to do with my grief. I wasn't a family member but I'd worked at Ground Zero. If I met the eye of a woman who'd lost her husband, or a son his father, I would find myself thinking, *Was that your husband's hand I blessed? Was that your father's torn shirt?* I dreamt of trying to put people back together again, of returning their limbs to them, but I was never able to.

I was unusually heavy-hearted when I came home from the memorial service. The turnout had been small, and the service felt dominated by local politicians who took turns at the microphone. No one wanted to be the person who did *not* speak. I was asked to give an invocation, though I would rather have shared a few simple words. To me, an invocation usually feels like a strange exercise: is it a prayer or just a call to order, a formality or a brief warm-up to whatever event is happening?

As I spoke, I suppose I was trying to invoke the broken heart of God, as well as God's hands, which hold all of our broken parts. My invocation was equal parts lament and petition. In some ways, it reflected what I was feeling about my experiences at Ground Zero: God didn't need an invitation to be present with us. God was already there. So did the invocation matter or was it merely an exercise to somehow make me (and those assembled) feel better? Likewise, the shattered remains of the victims did not need my—or any other—blessing. Long before the fractured pieces of their bodies reached the morgue, the souls of those who died were being held and blessed in far bigger hands than mine. *Did it mean anything, God?* I wondered after the memorial. *Did your children know their bodies were blessed . . . or were the blessings to remind we who remain that life is meaningful and worth living, and that we will not be forgotten when we die?*

My tearful conversation with God was suddenly interrupted by my son's excited voice. "Hey, Mom—come look at this. You'll never believe it." He was standing by a window that looks out onto our backyard. Darkness had fallen, but a single green light glowed along the fence.

"How can this be?" I whispered, shaking my head in awe. The light was coming from one of three flower-shaped solar lamps that we had hung in the spring. They had stopped working in mid-July, but we had left them there as decoration. In the evenings, we would sometimes remark that it was too bad they hadn't lasted very long and maybe we should try to fix them, but we never got around to it. The long days of summer and the abundance of sunlight made us lazy. But now, inexplicably, one was glowing as if it were brand-new—a green orb floating in a sea of darkness.

"Mom . . . I think that's for you," my son said. "I think the people you blessed are saying thank you."

"Maybe," I replied, putting my arm around him. "Or maybe the message is that God sees and remembers everything."

The light on the fence glowed for the next week, as if to reassure us that it wasn't some sort of fluke. At the end of the seven days, it went dark and stayed that way until we eventually replaced it with another the following spring.

Some might call it a coincidence, the sudden illumination of a light that had not been working, but I felt in it a blessing. On that anniversary of September 11, I had questioned so much. My soul was weary and, like the light, had grown dim. When the light began to glow again, I took it as a symbol of God's abiding presence—a gift. But what I also treasured was the fact that my son noticed it, and that his tender heart saw meaning in it—not for himself, but for me. It wasn't just "cool" that the light had come on; it had, in his mind, come on for a reason. It was an expression of recognition and gratitude. His mom's work had been meaningful. It was appreciated by forces he could not see but trusted were real. And because he believed this, so could I. Perhaps that was the real gift: the unbroken reflection of light from the fence to my son to me and back to the Divine. We formed a humming circuit of love, and we were recharged.

Hope

Against all hope, Abraham in hope believed.[5]

"Please don't tell Mom she's on hospice," the woman pleads, her wide brown eyes searching mine for reassurance. "We don't want to take away her hope."

"OK," I say, nodding, as she points me in the direction of the bedroom. I take a deep breath, aware of the fine line I am being asked to walk between honoring the family's request and the patient's right to know what is happening to her. After giving a soft tap on the door, I peek into the elderly woman's room. She greets me with a warm, mostly toothless smile and welcomes me in with a gentle wave of her hand. Then she motions for me to shut the door and to come closer.

I take a seat next to the bed, where she is comfortably propped up on pillows, and manage to introduce myself without using the word "hospice." Her eyes are kind and wise, and I get the feeling that she is participating in the usual polite chitchat solely for my benefit. Then she takes my hand and says, softly and tenderly, "Please don't tell my family that I'm dying. They are so hoping that I will get better."

The family who'd sought to protect their dying mother from despair by not telling her the truth about her illness had misunderstood: their

---

5   Romans 4:18, New International Version.

mother's hope was not based on getting better. She knew that her illness would be a temporary thing at best. Instead, she hoped that her family would not suffer too much when she died, and that she would be reunited with her loved ones in the world to come. Her hope was forward reaching, transcending the parameters of this life. Over the next two months, she would teach this to them—a final parting gift from a wise and loving woman.

"Let them know that I know," she said upon my next visit, "and that I want to talk about dying. Tell them I am not afraid." Gently conveying this to her family, I encouraged them to openly share with her their sadness over the thought of losing her, and to express their gratitude for all that she meant to them. In subsequent visits, after the air was cleared and they no longer needed me to serve as an intermediary, the tears and the laughter flowed freely. What I offered then was a fresh set of ears into which they could pour the stories of their lives. In doing so, important moments were lifted up, like gemstones to the light, where they could be cherished and marveled at anew. As a family, they looked back, celebrating all that had already been, but they also began to look forward. And here is where the elderly mother took them by the hand, emotionally and spiritually: "I've been here long enough," she said. "It's time for me to go home. I'm ready." As she grew weaker, sleeping more and eating less, her hopes and those of her family began to synchronize. Instead of hoping for her to get better, or hoping to spare her the reality of dying, the family tenderly and gratefully wished her well. They imagined her joyful reunion with those who had gone before her, and they whispered encouragement in her ear when she was no longer able to respond. In essence, they embraced her hope for a peaceful passing from this world to the next, and her promise that she had given all she could and had taught them all she knew about living and dying.

To have hope is essential to being human. It pulls us forward in difficult times; it keeps our spirits moving. When our hopes are dashed, however, as they sometimes are, we are challenged to go deeper, discovering instead the kind of hope that does not rely on outcomes or prayers being answered in the way that we had wanted. This is the kind of hope the dying woman embodied. She had shifted her gaze from the random and unpredictable events that make up a life to the unchangeable, eternal promise of God's love for her. She accepted the path that was unfolding, and she trusted that all would be well—with her soul and with the souls she left behind. That kind of hope can never be dashed by circumstance or by how life plays out.

True hope is a flower that grows from within. The seed is hidden in our DNA, buried in the very fabric of our human existence. It is how we are made. Just as the flower reaches for the sun, so our innermost souls reach for God. Even if we turn away, even if we refuse to acknowledge God, I believe we know. Deep down, we know. We have an intuitive awareness of the Divine because we come from the Divine. When God breathed into us the breath of life, we received something of God's essence. Our lungs filled with hope and with the promise that we would one day find our way back to the Home of our spirits. True hope, not hope based on wishful thinking or protectiveness or fear, is imperishable; it cannot be tarnished or extinguished by what may come in life. It is not stagnant or based on outcomes. It is fluid, moving with us, filling the spaces between what we envision for the future and what actually transpires. It is the safety pin that attaches us to God and reminds us that we are loved—no matter what.

It's not wrong to hope for things: for our children to be safe, for our loved ones to be happy and healthy, for our planet to know peace. These hopes run in my prayers on a continual loop. Consciously and unconsciously, I pray every day for these things. I hope for these things. But I also pray for the faith and the strength to bear the pain that is sure to come when things don't turn out the way I'd hoped. Few of us can escape the feeling of devastation when our prayers seem to go unanswered. Discovering the hard way that even the strongest among us cannot control every outcome, that even the most religious cannot guarantee a life free from suffering, can be a daunting realization.

I have hoped and prayed fervently for things that have not materialized. I have been devastated by loss and by disappointment. I have looked to the heavens with tears streaming down my face, wondering if it's all for nothing. But it is in these times that I have found a deeper sense of God's presence. Eventually, when I stop crying, when I have uncurled my fists and emptied my hands of everything that I have held on to, I discover that God has not emptied her hands of me. I am still held. I am still loved. God is no less divine, no less present, than before life knocked me to my knees. Because of what I have seen and experienced, I do not ask why things happen anymore, I ask only for the strength to endure what comes. I still reach for hope, but it is grounded in the promise that we do not walk through the valley alone; we are accompanied by the One who made us. Without this, my hope would be nothing more than wishful thinking.

For me, an essential facet of hope is one that I learned from my father—my spiritual mentor, guide, and friend. From the time I was small, the verse I most heard my dad repeat was this fragment from Colossians 1:27: "Christ in you, the hope of glory."[6] Dad always emphasized the *you*. It was so personal to him, so vitally important to him, and he thought that it was the most precious and crucial gift that he could give to us, which of course it was. The verse suggests that a great mystery is being revealed here, a secret is being shared, and the apostle Paul can hardly contain himself with wonder over it. "Christ in you" means that this part of God is within us, that God is not *out there*, somewhere far away or left for dead on a cross, but carried within us, not metaphorically but mysteriously and concretely. The Christ Spirit within acts as a homing device for the soul. It draws us to the Divine and takes the shape of hope. It is the Christ in us that recognizes the suffering Christ

---

6   New International Version.

in the poor and the hurting, the imprisoned and the bereft. If our hope is based on what is within us rather than what is around us, then it cannot be crushed by circumstance.

As a hospice chaplain, I try to bring something of God's compassionate presence to my patients. What I hope for them privately may be different from what they hope for themselves, but I always try to respect the faith and/or philosophy of my patients, as well as the boundaries of my role. For example, I recently had a seventy-three-year-old patient who had been estranged from her three adult children for several years. The patient, a very intelligent woman, had a long history of mental illness. She spent her early years in a Jewish refugee camp in Russia, was an atheist, and was recently divorced from her husband of forty-five years. When I met her, she told me that she had no use for spiritual care and did not want to talk about her children. I hoped, of course, for the possibility of reconciliation. After treading lightly for two weeks, I offered gentle support. Then the woman told me that she was afraid.

"What are you afraid of?" I asked her.

"I'm afraid of dying and I'm afraid of never seeing my children again." At this, she let out a wail that was almost primal in its pain.

Two days later, her children were located and within hours were traveling to be by her side. I believe she had been afraid to hope—afraid to hope that they would actually come, afraid to hope for what would happen if they did, afraid to hope that she would live long enough to see them. But come they did, immediately and lovingly. The beauty of that reconciliation will stay with me long after I can remember their names. If I had inserted *my* hope for the patient, she never would have been able to acknowledge or to verbalize hers.

In working with the terminally ill and their families, I am careful to be neither a "hope dangler" nor a "hope crusher." This was hard in the beginning. I had to learn to sit with the broken without trying to fix them, to lean into the jagged edges of grief with those who were bravely facing their mortality, and to be honest with myself about my own beliefs, my own fears. In essence, I had to go to the well and hash it out with God. What I heard God saying is this: Be a bearer of hope or, better yet, a *sharer* of hope. This doesn't mean making false promises; it means offering the assurance that we are all loved and no one is or will be forgotten. Love ignites the lamp of hope. As Meister Eckhart wrote, "What keeps us alive, what allows us to endure? I think it is the hope of loving, or being loved."

Hope is an innate part of being human, but life can bring such heartache that we may lose it for a time. We can help others rekindle their hope by being present, by listening, by acting with kindness and compassion, and by affirming the sacred worth of the individual. While we cannot necessarily instill hope in another person, we can hope *for* them temporarily. I experienced this myself when I was undergoing treatment for cancer. On a particularly bad day, when I was feeling pretty sorry for myself, I blurted out to a friend that I didn't want to be brave anymore. She responded, "You don't have to be. I will be brave for you." Hearing that, I felt such a wave of relief. I was not alone! I didn't have to be brave alone, believe alone, hope alone. I was being carried in a basket of love. I was baby Moses floating on the Nile, while loving eyes followed me to safety.

I have kept this experience with me, and it continues to teach me. For example, I once ran into a woman who lost her dog quite suddenly. Adding to her grief was the fact that she had recently survived a serious cancer diagnosis, with that dog at her side. Her canine companion offered more comfort than she could express, and his unexpected death left her devastated. "I prayed and I prayed," she sobbed. "I was a very religious person and now I want to take all my crosses and religious icons down. I'm so angry at God!"

Remembering my own experience, I told her, "You can be angry, Claudia. You can shake your fist at God. Let those of us who love you carry you for a while. Rest. Heal. We are a community of believers; chances are, you will be called to believe for someone else someday." The pain in her face began to ease and I could see her exhale. To feel happy and at peace in the world, we need to feel loved, and that whatever happens, our souls will be OK. Truly, we can carry one another in love, we can carefully hold the broken heart of another in hope.

Love for another person gives us the strength to hope. Love for God gives us the faith to keep going. We cannot choose the things that happen to us, but we always have the freedom to choose our response to what life brings. Like an advent calendar, where each window is opened one day at a time to reveal a gift, life holds hidden surprises that are waiting to be uncovered. We can't force ourselves to feel connected to God, but we can open the window. We can open our hearts to the possibility.

When I am weary, acts of kindness that I witness or experience are like water for my thirsty soul. They are a reminder that we do not have to carry our burdens alone. In fact, sometimes it is we who are carried on our mats, lowered in baskets, lifted to the well. Meanwhile, nature continues to sing its hymn of restoration with each new crocus that pushes through the cold earth, each bird that retraces its long journey home after winter, each wag of a dog's tail that emanates unconditional love. When we are filled with gratitude, we are filled with hope.

Mother to Mother

I was staring into the darkness beyond my window as the underground train rocked along, when a crumpled blue note was held between my eyes and infinity. "I'm from Bosnia," it began. Without reading the rest, I followed the hand attached to the arm attached to the person who held it: a woman—young, dark-eyed—with a baby strapped to her chest.

Such women were a familiar presence on the London trains during the time in which my husband and I lived there. Exiled Madonnas, almost always armed with children, they were an uncomfortable reminder of the sea of immigrants marching across the continent of Europe—marching, marching to yet another variation on the theme of poverty and displacement. After catching a glimpse of this woman boarding the train at the previous stop, I had readied some change in my hand to avoid any embarrassing shuffle of coins, lest the jingle in my pocket, like a telltale heart, reveal my selfishness.

I suppose I shouldn't have been startled, but by the time she and her note reached me I was far away, lost in some other world, some other thought buried in the blackness of the tunnel wall speeding by. For a split second, the note floated in that abyss between my eyes and the window—then my brain snapped into focus, and I remembered the coins pressed in my palm. A quick meeting of the eyes, and I released about thirty pence into her hand.

She moved on.

Usually, I would have returned to my insulated ponderings, but this time I felt alert, like someone who's been shaken from a deep sleep. Blood coursed through my veins at a slightly accelerated pace; the animal in me raised my head and pawed the ground with nostrils flaring.

I watched as she held her note, steadily, methodically, in front of one nose after another. There was neither hope nor hopelessness apparent in her gesture, but rather something between resignation and resolve, humility and grace. I watched as, one by one, each head shook in refusal, the faces puckering in and growing cold. It was like watching candles being extinguished in the windows of a house just before the shutters slam shut.

When her pass through the car was complete, the final denial given, something within me groaned. *Why shouldn't we give her money? Would a few pence even be missed?* I was both relieved not to be one of *them* and ashamed at my own reflection in those faces. I knew all the good reasons for refusing: you can't give to everyone . . . this sort of thing shouldn't be encouraged . . . it's an intrusion. But still. Still. If only the others in the car had seen her.

The train slowed to a stop in a tunnel between stations, and the young woman found a seat on which to rest, diagonally across from me. She had slim, supple hands and long dark hair that was pulled back into a loose braid. On the round head of the sleeping baby was a tiny knit hat. I noticed that it was worn, but not dirty—in fact, it was immaculate. The same went for his clothes. Try as I might, I could not take my eyes away from mother and child. They were a humming, impenetrable unit. *Incarnation* was the word that kept coming to me. *When love incarnates, it must look something like this,* I thought. The woman stroked the baby's sleeping face, tenderly caressing his brow and lingering over the curve of his forehead. She gently wiped an invisible smudge from his cheek, seemingly oblivious to the presence of anyone else on the train. For her, there was only him—this moment and then the next, existing as backdrop to his perfection.

A pound coin burned in my pocket. How to give it to her? And why hadn't I given it in the first place? It wasn't much, but it was about all I had with me. I glanced at the passengers on either side of me. The idea of handing it across the laps and space between us seemed awkward and embarrassing. Maybe I should just forget it. Maybe it was too little too late.

The train began moving again, pulling into the next station. The woman with the baby was standing by the doors now, preparing to get off. Without thinking, I jumped up and followed her as the doors opened and closed. She was moving swiftly in front of me, gracefully weaving through the bodies on the platform. Without knowing what else to do, I caught up with her and tapped her on the shoulder. She turned, eyebrows raised in detached curiosity, and then her eyes met mine. Awkwardly, I held out my coin, gave a little shrug, and felt my cheeks flush.

Her hand came out slowly, automatically, but her eyes remained fixed on mine. Finally, she glanced down, closed her hand around the coin, and met my gaze again. When she did, something had changed. The world was balanced for a moment. The circular flow of energy had shifted to allow me in, and we stood there smiling without saying a word. Her eyes were warm and rich like the color of the earth, and her face was radiant and kind. Then, quieter than a whisper, the words "Thank you" formed on her lips.

We parted and walked to opposite ends of the long platform. I could hear the faint tinkling of coins as she counted her day's earnings. Then the tears came, without much warning, sliding down my cheeks in little rivers, like droplets of rain against a window. I wasn't even sure why. All I knew was that something had happened to me, something audible only to nature, some flame ignited against a cave wall.

A few days later, I discovered that I was pregnant with my first child. As I placed my hands on my belly, I thought of the woman on the train. It was December. Angels, stars, and crèches were everywhere. Once again, the holy family was traveling, traveling, traveling—through Advent, through time and space—homeless and weary and left to rely on the kindness of strangers. The irony did not escape me. In every Madonna, I saw the face of the woman on the train, the blue of Mary's robe shimmering like the paper note that first shook me from my sleep.

Perhaps it was the mystery of life growing within and beyond me that recognized the same within and beyond her. The same Pulse that set the world in motion was pulsing now in me, moving me to respond to a frequency I couldn't hear with my ears but could feel in my blood. Like Mary and Elizabeth, we touched hands and our babies leapt. *I know you. I know you,* they called. *You are kin to me.*

But before I could begin to grasp what my heart already intuited, the next train came and I boarded. A moment later, another dark-eyed woman made her way up the aisle with another dark-eyed baby, and another tattered piece of paper. I shook my bag, sifting through its contents for one more coin. And when she came to me, I smiled and paid her homage.

Jimmy's Home

The doctors told us that he died from complications relating to a stroke, but I think it would be more accurate to say that my brother died from complications relating to Vietnam, which began some forty-five years earlier. Although the war was many years ago, I can honestly say that he was never the same afterward.

Jimmy joined the army soon after he turned eighteen. He knew his draft number would be coming up and thought he'd be better off as an enlisted man. He served two tours of active duty in a place that must have felt as far from Ohio as Dante's Inferno.

I was six years old the day he left for the service. It was 1967 and the war was raging. "I thought we weren't supposed to fight," I said, blinking up at my parents as they tried to explain where he was going and why. The looks on their faces and the seriousness in their voices frightened me. Suddenly, the large duffle bag that was slumped against the wall looked menacing. It was taking my brother away to a place that was dangerous and scary, a place I couldn't understand. My two older sisters and I listened outside the kitchen as my parents gave their last, furtive instructions, as if words could protect Jimmy. I caught a glimpse of my mother's upturned face, her expression one of fierce protection and unspoken fears. I had never seen her look like that. My father's hand was resting on Jimmy's shoulder, and I could see that he was praying, his closed eyes managing somehow to emanate beams of light.

When they came out of the kitchen, Jimmy bent down to hug each of us good-bye. He was tall and fluid, his playful smile still in place, still properly attached to that eighteen-year-old face. "Be good," he told us, before slinging the duffle over his shoulder and walking out the door. We watched from the window as my father drove him toward a place from which there would be no emotional return.

Because of Jimmy, the Vietnam War was more real for me than for many children my age. I was the only first grader I knew who had a brother fighting in the war. My family prayed for him around the dinner table each evening and on our knees before going to bed each night. We talked about him a lot, tethering him to us in the only way we could. Perhaps my mom wanted to make sure we didn't forget him, in case he didn't come back. Talking about Jimmy kept him vivid and current in our day-to-day lives.

Sitting at the kitchen table as my mom prepared dinner, I would write him letters. Once in a while, I would get one back. Holding one of Jimmy's letters in my small hands was like holding a magic, invisible thread. The thin paper would be wrinkled and smeared with dirt, and there would be no postal stamp, but the handwriting meant that he had actually been at the other end of it. Touching the letter was almost like touching him. In it, he would usually ask how I was doing in school, and he might tell me about the weather in that faraway place. "It rains a lot," I remember him writing. His words were warm and sweet. The only indication of danger was one letter that ended abruptly with "Got to go!" Mom frequently sent him packages of food and necessities, never knowing whether they would actually reach him. For his nineteenth birthday, she baked him a cake. I remember watching her carefully wrap it in layers and layers of cellophane before packing it in a box with a card and some other small things.

"Won't it be stale by the time he gets it?" we asked her.

"Maybe," she had replied, "but he'll know we were thinking of him and we remembered his birthday."

The day Jimmy came home from Vietnam, it was summertime. My sisters and I had hung a paper banner across the front of the house with the words *Welcome Home Jimmy* sprawled in colorful markers. Mom made his favorite foods, including the same kind of cake she'd sent on his birthday. Our parents had offered to throw a small party for him with family and close friends, but he had politely declined. They chalked this up to the fact that he had always been rather shy. Never could we have fathomed it was because a part of him had died.

I remember positioning myself at the window to watch for him. Even though I hadn't seen him for two years, his image loomed large in my mind. He was the tall, skinny brother, the one who could rescue me if I found myself stuck in a tree, which I did on more than one occasion. The last time this happened was just before he left. Clinging to a branch like a kitten who's climbed too high, I cried out—not for my mother, not for my father, but for Jimmy. I called and called his name until the patio door slid open. With tears streaming down my face, I watched as he took long, deliberate strides, crossing the expanse between our back door and the tree in record time. He was shaking his head a little, as if annoyed, but as he reached for me his eyes were laughing and a sweet smile curled the corner of his lips. I let go of the branch and slid into the safety of his extended arms. Instead of just plopping me back down onto the grass, he gently carried me into the house, my arms wrapped tightly around his neck, my head on his shoulder, my tears dampening his shirt. I was safe.

Now my rescuer and hero was coming home. But when he walked through the door, I remember thinking, *Something's wrong. Where's Jimmy? What have they done with him?* It was his face and his body, but *he* was missing. I wanted to run to him, to be swept up into the safety of those arms again, but I suddenly felt shy because I could not find him. Eyes that once sparkled with the humor and confidence of an athletic teenager were now haunted and hollow. What followed for Jimmy were struggles with depression, with alcohol, with homelessness, and with demons I will never be able to fathom. Over the next forty-some years, I would catch only glimpses of the brother I'd known those first precious years of my life.

We never know what life may have in store for us. We cannot anticipate the joy, much less the challenges or the hardships. So how are we to live? How are we to prepare for all we cannot know? The US Army called Jimmy to fight a battle he did not start and could not fully anticipate. Jimmy's conscience prompted him to respond to that call— and then haunted him with what he'd been required to do. It seems an unfair proposition. The personal battles that he continued to face were exacerbated by the derision and disrespect he and so many other Vietnam vets encountered upon their return, deepening the psychic wounds left by the war.

After the Vietnam War, my brother did not know who he was. Was he the "baby killer" some accused him of being? Was he the "idiot" who went to Vietnam instead of Canada? Or was he the kid from Ohio, the shy son, the big brother who carried his sisters in his arms? He didn't know anymore. And who was God? Was God some indifferent witness to the horrific battlefield deaths of his buddies, or was God the listening ear to our mother's constant prayers for his protection?

One of the few stories that he shared with my parents about his time in Vietnam had to do with the power of those prayers. Jimmy described how, in the midst of one of the most intense battles, he witnessed his best friend getting blown out of a watchtower, his body on fire and torn apart. Bullets were flying; the cries of the wounded and the dying could be heard all around him. Eight of the twenty-four men in his squad would die that day—and yet it was as if a protective shield had been wrapped around him. While shells whizzed past his helmet and explosions ripped the earth, he heard my mother's voice praying the Psalm she had sent him, the one she prayed every day, multiple times a day:

A thousand may fall at your side, ten thousand at your
right hand, but it will not come near you.[7]

He felt certain that those prayers had saved him.

Jimmy had survived physically, but the bullets he could not dodge
were the ones that continued to haunt his dreams and shred his identity.
Like Humpty Dumpty, my brother was broken and I did not know how
to put him back together again. My arms were never long or strong
enough to reach him, to pluck him from whatever branch he was clinging to in his mind, nor could I carry him to safety. Even if I could have,
I know that he would have slipped from my hands because one cannot
carry a ghost.

Perhaps now, from a higher vantage point, Jimmy can see how
much he was loved. Free from depression, from mental illness, and from
the nightmares that haunted him, he might recognize the ways in which
God accompanied him throughout his life. Like the prodigal son, he
was always welcomed back into the family with open arms, no matter
how many times he disappeared. After he'd been homeless and missing
for years, he was found when a niece somehow recognized him in the
gaunt, bearded man standing on the corner holding a sign that read,
Hungry Vet. When he was again lost to his illness and facing homelessness, a kind stranger reached out to him. The man's brother had been a
veteran who had taken his own life, and he saw something of his brother
in mine. It was he who brought Jimmy to the hospital after the stroke,
he who asked Jimmy for permission to call the family. Because of this
stranger's compassion, Jimmy did not die alone but was surrounded by
his family in a circle of love. The fact that his was a difficult life does not
mean he was forgotten by God. "In this world you will have trouble,"
Jesus said. "But take heart! I have overcome the world."[8]

---

7   Psalm 91:7, New International Version.
8   John 16:33, New International Version.

When I pass a soldier in an airport or on the street, I think of Jimmy. When I see them in homecoming videos wrapping their arms around their surprised children or laughing with their faithful dogs, I pray that they remember who they are. The emotional beauty of those first hellos, the initial euphoria, will soon be replaced by everyday struggles. The uniforms will come off but they will have left a mark. Sometimes that mark obscures the fact that they are the same babies who were once held and loved. They are the brothers and sisters who teased and rescued, played and argued. They are mothers and fathers, sons and daughters. They are God's unique masterpieces.

The Great Architect has designed each of our blueprints. As such, they are impermeable, inflammable, and eternal. Life can tatter us, it can shatter us, but it cannot change the fact that we are loved. Our very souls bear a divine microchip. Each day of our lives, and with each beat of our hearts, the soul searches for direction. We are never truly lost. Even if we have no idea who or where we are, God always knows how to find us . . . and God's arms are always long and strong enough to reach us. The sooner we call for help, the sooner we will feel God's presence. In life, Jimmy was never alone, despite his struggles and his sorrow. In death, he let go of the branch but he did not fall. God gently carried him from the tree, saying, "Come on, son, let's go home."

The Blessing

"To give someone a blessing is the most significant affirmation we can offer."
—*Henri Nouwen*

Sitting across from Catherine in her cozy apartment, I almost forget that she is dying. We've been chatting about the birthday party her family threw for her the day before. "I was just getting ready to go to bed when I heard a knock on the door. It was only about seven thirty, but I'm *old*," she says, laughing. When I protest, saying that eighty-five doesn't seem that old to me, at least not on her, she cocks her head to one side and says, "Talk to me when you get there, baby." Catherine is what one would call a straight shooter. Petite and elegant, smart and warm, she is both deeply religious and hilariously profane. In short, she is my type of girl. She has survived breast cancer, multiple strokes, congestive heart failure, and the loss of her oldest son at the age of fifty. Even in her diminished state, she is a formidable force. Strongly connected to her Greek heritage and to her orthodox church, she has the ability to look unflinchingly toward the future—which includes the certainty that she is going to die soon—while remaining squarely grounded in the present.

Although I enjoy visiting Catherine, part of me always dreads it. Not because the visit is sad or unpleasant—quite the contrary. I dread it because I love her, and loving her means that I will have my heart broken when she dies. It is unavoidable. Her hospice nurse, Maggie, feels the same way. Although we offer loving care to all of our patients, there are some with whom you make a special connection. Catherine is one of those people. She has a way of remaining utterly herself, without letting her illness eclipse her personality and spirit. And this is no small miracle. Though mostly confined to a wheelchair and unable to open her left eye, she exudes a vibrancy that is magnetic. Her smile is wide and playful, and she has the softest skin imaginable. Whenever I take her hand it always surprises me with its supple silkiness, and I never fail to tell her so.

After sharing about her impromptu birthday party, she turns her attention to me. "So how are you, baby? What's going on?" With some people, especially when it's a patient or a patient's family member, one can answer such a question in a cursory way. The person who is asking is often just trying to be polite or is anxious to shift the conversation from talk of death to something else. Mundane conversation can provide a needed distraction for someone whose world is consumed by illness. When Catherine asks me how I am, however, she really wants to know. "Tell me and don't give me any bulls—t," she says with a laugh.

I have been a hospice chaplain long enough to know that I am not there to solicit her support, nor is it appropriate to burden her with my issues. At the same time, to deny Catherine the dignity of being able to offer her wisdom and her concern would also be dismissive and patronizing. It is a fine line that we must learn to walk as professionals, and I do a quick self-evaluation of my motives before answering her. The truth is, I *do* have something going on. I am scheduled for surgery in the morning, and I am facing it with no small measure of trepidation. The surgery is yet another reconstructive procedure, one that is related to my breast cancer of several years ago. I would not normally be so nervous about it, but the last such surgery I had (three months ago) almost killed me. People have told me that I am crazy for returning to the clinic where a medical error almost did me in, but the surgeon is renowned and the error was the nurse anesthetist's, not his. Still, I am terrified of what might happen . . . of what almost did happen.

Before the visit, I had planned on letting Catherine know that I would not be coming at our usual time the following week, but I hadn't intended to spill the beans on why. Trying to sound breezy, I tell her that I am having an outpatient procedure in the morning. "Nothing to worry about," I say, with a wave of my hand. She studies me for a moment, and I know she's not buying my feigned nonchalance. Leaning forward in her wheelchair, she focuses that one good eye on me. It's like a searchlight that has suddenly pinned a runaway in place. I start to squirm under her gaze.

"Hey, hold on a minute," she says in a tone that is both concerned and serious. "What gives?"

Knowing I have to elaborate, I tell her about the procedure and why I am scared. We have the deep bond of being breast cancer survivors, and I can feel her immediate care for me as one who has been there. As we talk, she is no longer the eighty-five-year-old patient in the wheelchair; she is my wise confidant, embodying the heart of my mother, my grandmother, my sister, my friend. She listens intently without saying a word. I know she is taking it all in, what I say and what I fail to say. She looks to me like a raven about to take flight, her head cocked to one side, the bright blackness of her right eye reminiscent of the night sky.

"You are going to be fine," she declares finally, her voice fierce. I am both startled and silenced by her pronouncement. It's the feeling you get when you are stopped in your tracks by the sound of a branch snapping somewhere in the woods. You pause to listen with a particular stillness. "You're going to be fine," she says again, this time more softly. She does not say this as a platitude. There is no hint of pandering or denial in her voice, as if she does not grasp the texture of my fear. She is not dismissive. Her words feel like an official proclamation. She has declared that I will be fine, and I *will* be, as if there were no other option. She has struck the gavel and released me from the imprisonment of worry. Why? *Because I will be fine.*

I thank her for her words of encouragement before trying to turn the subject back to her, but she will have none of it. Raising a wizened finger, she says, "Wait. I have something for you." Before I can get a word of protest out, she turns and starts paddling over to her desk. It is not an easy task for her. She leans forward in the wheelchair as if facing off against a strong wind.

"You know I can't take anything from you," I say to the back of her small, curled body. She waves me off and tells me to be quiet. "Stay there," she says over her shoulder. Once at her desk, Catherine begins to carefully lift and move things around—letters, books, a framed picture of a saintly icon. "Ah," she says, retrieving a small wooden jewelry box. Although it doesn't play a tune when she opens the lid, I feel the music of secret things escape from it. She tenderly thumbs through the contents, then a smile lights her face. "Here it is," she says, closing her hand around a small object.

I walk over to her, conscious of the ease with which I have just crossed the same expanse. There is no headwind for me, no strain, but the strength of spirit that Catherine is exuding eclipses my physical advantage. Humbled, I kneel down next to her.

"What I'm going to give you is very holy," she whispers, gesturing carefully with her cupped hands. It's almost as if she holds a hummingbird or a butterfly, something that will fly away once she opens her hands. She leans down, her face mere inches from mine. "Not only did I get this from Jerusalem, but I laid it on the tomb of the Holy Sepulchre, the tomb of Jesus."

"Cath—" I start to protest. But before I can finish, she uncups her hands, revealing a small silver crucifix no more than two inches long. Attached to the top is a tiny crimson cushion in the shape of a diamond, with a gold tassel. It takes my breath away—not because it is the most beautiful thing I have seen but because of the energy it emanates.

"I can't take this, Catherine," I protest.

"Oh, you're taking it," she replies firmly, pressing it into my hand. "I don't want an argument."

"It's stunning," I tell her. "Simply stunning—and magical. I can feel the Divine vibrations coming off this . . . but Catherine, I can't take it from you. I can't. Why don't you just hold it when you pray for me. Or let me hold it for a few minutes now, and I will soak in its blessing."

I shut my eyes and cup my hands around the crucifix, the way I'd seen Catherine do. I feel my hands growing warm, and I quiet my mind and spirit to receive its blessing, along with Catherine's. When I open my eyes, I offer the cross back to Catherine, but she blocks my hand.

"I want you to know that this cross is not only from Jerusalem, and not only did it touch the tomb of Christ, it was also blessed. As I laid the cross on that tomb, three monks happened to walk by. And so I asked them to bless it, which they did. So, you see, this cross is triply blessed. It is very, very holy."

I express, again, how genuinely touched I am that she would want me to have it, but I am unwavering in my refusal to accept such a gift from her. We're in a battle of wills, a humorous reverse tug-of-war over the cross. She is adamant that I take it; I am firm in my refusal. Finally, I say, "What if we compromise? What if I take the cross with me to my surgery and then return it when it's over. That way, you can share it with someone else who might need it someday. Unfortunately," I continue, "we will always have people in our lives who need a little extra blessing."

Squinting at me, she seems to be weighing this in her mind. Then she says, "OK, deal."

"Deal," I answer with a relieved smile, as I give her a hug.

When I start to pull away, however, she doesn't let go. Instead, she holds on tight and begins fervently whispering a prayer. Her cheek is pressed against mine and her warm breath is in my ear. I'm startled by the strength of her embrace. She holds me tightly, as if I might run away before she is through. Her words are flowing like a river. And somehow the image that comes to mind is that of the Annunciation of Mary, with the words of the Holy streaming into her ear. Catherine's words are streaming, too, as if channeled from the Divine. She is praying for my safety, praying for my health, and she is asking the angels to surround me and keep me safe. There is an urgency and fervor in her voice. When she finally pauses, I pray, too. I give thanks for Catherine, for her friendship and her wisdom, her prayers and her generosity. And I ask God to sustain her on this final part of her journey. She offers one more blessing and we remain entwined, me kneeling on the floor and she in her wheelchair.

When she releases me, tears are streaming down my face, and she looks exhausted, as if this has taken every bit of energy out of her.

"You've really touched me, Catherine," I say, wiping my eyes. "I'm supposed to be here helping *you*."

"No, baby," she answers, shaking her head, "we are here to help each other. And remember," she continues in her gravelly voice, "JC's got your back. You hear me? JC always has your back. Just put your faith in him and everything will be fine. That's the only thing that sustains me—and it will sustain you."

After she says this, I notice that Catherine looks small and pale, and has slumped down in her chair. When I gently mention that she looks tired, she agrees, saying, "Yes, I should probably lie down now." At that, her caregiver glides over, without making a sound, and turns the wheelchair toward the bedroom.

I stand watching until they disappear, then I turn to leave, a pocketful of holiness carried with me as I go.

Spirit Daughter

It was unusual for me to be sitting at my desk at the hospice office in the middle of the afternoon. On most days, I was out visiting patients in the community at that time. But for a reason I can't remember—perhaps a patient had canceled or I had returned from a meeting—I happened to be in my little cubicle when the phone rang. I noticed it had been routed to me from the hospital. When I answered, the voice on the other end was soft and shaky, and clearly that of a young girl. "I'm interested in a bereavement group," she said, curling her last word in a way that made it more question than statement.

"Okaaay," I answered slowly, instinctively leaning forward in an effort to tune in to this unexpected frequency. I was well acquainted with the sound of sorrow on the other end of the telephone line, but this little voice took me by surprise. "Can I ask who it is that you are grieving?"

"My mom," said the girl, her throat thick with tears.

The words landed with a soft thud in the center of my chest. It was like getting hit at close range with a well-kicked soccer ball or a velvet-fisted punch meant for someone else. I took a quick gulp of air, readying myself for the sting that was sure to follow . . . then I exhaled as quietly as I could.

"How old are you, honey?"

"Fourteen."

Oh dear God, I thought. "When did your mom die?"

"Three years ago," she said, with a brokenness that she didn't try to hide.

My mind skipped first to the practical. The bereavement group that I was currently offering was for people who had lost a spouse or a partner. I don't think there was anyone under sixty-five. While made up of wonderful people, the group clearly wasn't going to work for this young girl.

"Well," I began, "I'm so glad that you called. It's very brave of you—but the group that I'm facilitating at the moment wouldn't really be a good fit for you. Do you have any family, anyone who is supportive?" I didn't want to assume anything about her.

"I have my dad," she said, in her sweet, singsongy voice. "And I'm actually a triplet."

A triplet. Images and memories began flashing through my mind, like the blur of cherries and lemons spinning on a slot machine. When they stopped, a little bell went off and it began to dawn on me that I might know the family to whom this girl belonged. How many triplets could there be within driving distance of the hospital, I reasoned, especially triplets whose mother had died?

"You're a triplet? Wow . . . do you also happen to have an older sister?" I asked.

"Yes," she sniffed.

"Is her name Niamh?"

"Yes . . ."

I paused, weighing my words before saying as gently as I could, "Honey, I knew your mom."

I had met Sorcha's mother some twelve years before receiving that call. It was on a bright-blue August day. I was walking to the local elementary school for kindergarten orientation with my son, Alex. A lazy breeze meandered through the trees, making shimmering tambourines of the leaves high above. Alex was holding my hand. I was acutely aware that I could still swoop him up and carry him in my arms if I wanted to. If I did, his strong cricket legs would lock around my back and his arms would clasp behind my neck. The fact that these days would soon be gone was cemented with each step toward the school. Perhaps that's one reason that day is so clear to me. I tried to take in each image so that I would remember the color of the sky, the feel of his hand, the look of his fine blond hair moving in little waves as we went along.

Coming from another direction, Sorcha's mom, Janet, was walking with Niamh. Our eyes met before our paths actually intersected, and we smiled a hello, communicating the way that mothers can without saying a word. I remember her dark straight hair and heavy bangs, her wide smile, and her clothes, which indicated that she was probably a professional of some sort rather than a stay-at-home mom. We walked into the building together, with our five-year-olds clinging shyly to our hands, and soon discovered that our kids were destined for the same classroom. Taking a seat next to one another, we introduced ourselves before turning our attention to the teacher.

Though it seems strange to say, it is only Janet whom I remember clearly from that day, even though I rarely saw her after that. She was a successful and respected architect in New York City, one who worked long hours and was usually unavailable for the routine dropping off and picking up of children. As the years unfolded, I became friendly with other moms with whom I also must have sat in the classroom on orientation day. Strangely, I do not remember any other first hellos . . . but I remember Janet's, even all these years later.

Sorcha's father, on the other hand, became a familiar figure as he shepherded Niamh back and forth to school, with three toddlers in tow. He was tall and lanky, quiet and shy, with friendly eyes and a lilting Irish accent. Because of Janet's schedule, he was home with the children during the day. Keeping track of triplets must have been a monumental task but he never appeared rattled. In response to the curious looks he would sometimes get as he walked with the toddlers tethered to safety harnesses, he would merely nod his head and smile.

Now, one of those floppy-haired triplets was a teenager, and she was crying on the other end of the phone. I closed my eyes and tried to find a clear image of the triplets, curious if I could pick Sorcha out from her two brothers, but the picture was hazy. They were all movement and overalls, a tumbling, giggling unit, with no awareness of the uniqueness of their birth. I didn't know their names. To me, they were just "the triplets," otherwise known as Niamh's little siblings.

It was nearly nine years after that first hello when I heard that Janet had died. Instead of August, it was June. Instead of the school year beginning, it was finally winding down. On that particular morning, I was in the park enjoying some quiet time with my dogs when another mother came toward me, her face drawn, her eyes broadcasting bad news. She was like a walking smoke signal coming over the hill. One look, and I knew there was trouble. "Did you hear what happened?" she asked, in a tone that spoke volumes. Without waiting for an answer, she blurted out, "Niamh's mom, Janet, died."

While the most contact I'd ever had with Janet was probably on that orientation day, my heart sank. Alex and Niamh had been in almost every class together since kindergarten, and they were about to graduate from middle school. Naturally, I felt shaken by the news, by the unavoidable reverberations and the unfixable nature of it all—and I also felt somewhat haunted. Janet was here and then gone, someone I knew but never knew. In the days to come, the community would rally. Food would be dropped off, cards and flowers sent, help offered. But nothing could mend the gaping hole left in that family, not even the best intentions.

The end of the school year opened the gates of summer, spilling kids into the community like roving packs of happy puppies. In addition to the kids in baseball uniforms and flip flops, I would occasionally see Niamh riding her bike down the street or stopping at the local pizzeria for a slice. She had a sweet, dreamy face that was hard to read. Whenever I asked my son how he thought Niamh was coping with the loss of her mom, he always shrugged and said she seemed OK. I wasn't sure how to reach out to Niamh's father without being intrusive, so I would ask about the family through people who were closer to them. In retrospect, I wish I had made more of an effort.

It's strange to say now, but I usually thought of Janet's death in terms of Niamh, in part because of the memory of that first meeting, and in part because although I had watched Niamh grow through the years, the triplets remained frozen in my mind as roly-poly toddlers.

But it wasn't Niamh who was now calling; it was Sorcha, one of the triplets. And she didn't even know it was *me* she was calling. From the girl's locker room at school, she had called the local hospital in search of a bereavement group. How she got the courage to do that, I will never know. After realizing who she was and explaining about the current group, I suggested that we meet for a walk after school. I knew the street where she lived and the direction she would be coming from, so we decided to just start walking from our houses and meet somewhere in the middle.

"I'll be walking my pug, Chester," I told her, "so you'll know who I am."

As Chester and I started down the street, I tried not to worry about what to say to Sorcha. What *could* I say? My heart broke for her, as it did for all children who have lost a parent. I thought of the hole left in my father's heart after his mother's death when he was nine years old. For the rest of his life, he carried what felt to me like a little silk pouch of tears next to his heart. When he died, he didn't have to carry it anymore. I imagined the cord unraveling and simply slipping from his neck. When the pouch opened, the tears were gone; they had been reabsorbed back into the heavens. I always wished someone had been there to help him when he was little or that there had been a way for me to ease his pain. Maybe that's why Sorcha's call touched me so. The sadness was familiar. Just because it couldn't be fixed didn't mean that it could not be eased.

So, our paths intersected, just as they had when I met Sorcha's mom. This time, walking toward me was a tall, willowy teenager. No longer an indistinguishable toddler, Sorcha was strikingly beautiful, with long chestnut hair and green-blue eyes the color of the sea. We walked to the park together, the same park where I had learned of her mom's death, and we sat on a hill looking out to the ocean. As she began to speak, Sorcha absentmindedly pulled up tufts of grass, dropping them in fluttery piles. It struck me that I had done the same thing, in nearly the same spot, when I was sitting with a friend after being diagnosed with cancer. Maybe we try to hold on to the Earth when it is spinning too fast, or maybe we are the grass, being torn from our roots. In any case, it's a way of not screaming or banging our heads on the ground when faced with what we cannot change.

As the months unfolded, I became one of a select few women whom Sorcha would come to call her "earth mamas" (because her real mom was in heaven, she reasoned), and she would become my "spirit daughter." I couldn't have anticipated the joy that Sorcha would bring into my life or the privilege of being one of her "earth mamas." Watching her grow into the strong, deeply spiritual young woman that she is has been an inspiration. She humbles me with her quest for meaning, her desire to be a healing presence in the world, and her resilient spirit. She is training to be a yoga instructor, is already a Reiki healer, and remains unpretentious, honest, and grounded. When she comes to church with me, she holds my hand, and I feel the connection to *her* mother and to every child who cannot hold her own mother's hand. What's more, I sense my father smile. It's as if he knows that I feel him in her hand. And I'm grateful. Something else mysterious has happened. The sadness that has lived beneath the surface of my skin since having had two miscarriages years ago has now dissipated. Along with the sorrow had been the secret feeling that I had more mothering to do. What I didn't understand then is that there are many ways to mother.

As Sorcha prepares to go off to college, I feel the same nervous anticipation I would if she were my own child. Incidentally, her sister, Niamh, is doing well. I don't see her often, but when I do, she smiles and I see her twirling on her mother's arm on that August day. Another mother has been *her* touchstone—one who lives nearby and who lost her only child in a tragic car accident. Thus, once more, we are brought to each other. More than ever, I am convinced that God does not cause terrible things to happen to us, but guides us, always toward comfort and healing.

"Ask and it will be given to you; seek and you will find; knock and the door will be opened to you,"[9] we are told in Matthew 7:7. Perhaps the key is to remain open to the surprising ways in which our prayers are answered. God did not seem to answer Sorcha's prayers to heal her mom, but God guided her to other hearts willing and able to mother her. Similarly, I do not believe that I was meant to have a miscarriage so that I could love Sorcha, but Sorcha's presence has allowed me to tap into a reservoir of love. Some would call it a lucky chance that Sorcha's call was routed to me that day and that I was there to receive it, but I know differently. Her mother and I met with one hand holding a child's and one hand open to the other. The secret lies in that open hand.

---

9   New International Version.

The Swan's Surrender

Before I knocked on Polly's door, I knew that she was dead. I knew it as I made my way to her along busy streets filled with cars, past children playing and people going about their lives. The world outside was immersed in time, which continues to flow unhindered by human events and indifferent to our dramas. I did not listen to the radio as I drove, and I did not make any cell phone calls; I just thought of her and of the last time we spoke. As I parked the car and walked up the stone steps of her apartment building, death accompanied me like an old friend. It walked beside me; it draped its silver-sleeved arm around my shoulders; it whispered in my ear, *Courage. All is well.*

The tap of my feet on the dark marble entryway echoed slightly as I stepped into the lovely prewar building. When the door shut behind me, the noise of the outside world was suddenly muted. I became aware of the soft, steady thump of my heart beating just under the surface of my skin, aware of my breath circulating, without effort, through my lungs. As I walked up the steps, I ran my fingers along the cool painted wall, absorbing the strength of the building. Whenever I visited, it would occur to me that this fortress could offer protection or imprisonment, safety or isolation, depending on its inhabitants. Today, however, it felt oddly neutral and empty, like a mausoleum.

Standing in the hallway, I paused to exhale, then I knocked softly on the heavy apartment door and let myself in. When I crossed the threshold, stillness enveloped me. It passed through my body in a millisecond, confirming what I already knew. One of Polly's daughters—tall, blonde, fortyish—glided toward me with the graceful elegance of a dancer. Her eyes were watery and her lips trembled a little as she smiled, but her demeanor was calm. "I'm so glad you're here," she whispered, opening her arms to embrace me. "Come. My sister is inside with Mom."

We walked down a long unlit hall into the late afternoon sun of the living room. The room was silent, as only a room inhabited by the dead can be. It was like walking into a painting. Katherine, Polly's eldest daughter, was sitting by her mother's bedside. She looked up at me and nodded a hello. Without speaking, I bent to hug her then stood with my hand on her shoulder, both of us gazing at the porcelain figure lying motionless in the bed.

"How are you doing?" I asked after a few minutes. A stupid question—simplistic, really—but it is how we begin.

"I'm OK," she answered, her voice steady and ringing true. "Mom was so ready to go. For the longest time she couldn't figure out why she was still here . . . but in the end, she was peaceful. Her breathing just sort of slowed down, and then it finally stopped."

I moved to the other side of the bed and took a seat across from Katherine. Polly lay between us in her hospital bed. It faced a large window with a view of a golf course. The bed had become the centerpiece of the elegant paneled living room, nudging aside the old grand piano that was now forced to stand like a stately matron in the corner. Irises and yellow tulips were in vases scattered around the room, softening the heavy molding, while the disembodied voice of a singer from the forties floated from a CD player. It lent a melancholy atmosphere to an apartment already saturated with things past.

I looked at Polly, at her smooth skin and at her face, now still as a stone. Maybe I was searching for some sign that she had at last found peace. It's not that she had led a tortured life, but she'd carried a great deal of remorse regarding her past, particularly the years when her five children were growing up. She was an alcoholic who'd only recently been in recovery. We used to brush the surface of this issue in our talks together, but she was never really willing to go there. Perhaps she was afraid that nothing could truly wedge her out of her guilt and shame. Instead, she became fixated on her anger toward God and toward the church. Why was this happening to her? Was God punishing her? Why couldn't her priest find a way to comfort her? Why could no one give her a decent answer to her questions of *why*? As she became more confused, she seemed to have forgotten what it was that had troubled her so. Anger turned into anguish over why she was still alive, and her perceived inability to "let go" became her new source of shame. *Why is it so hard to die?* she wondered. Had God forgotten her—or was *not* dying simply her latest failure? Each time I visited, she would look at me eagerly, her eyes begging me to reveal the secret that I was obviously withholding. And each time I left, I knew that she was disappointed.

"I hope you have found peace, Polly," I said into the strange expanse that separates the living from the dead. Katherine smoothed Polly's hair and stroked her arm. Then, leaning on the bed rails, she took her mother's limp hand and lifted it to her lips. As Katherine described the events of the last few hours, she gently tossed her mother's hand absentmindedly between her own, while gazing lovingly at her surrendered beauty. Polly's hand was still warm and supple, but the color was slowly draining from it, slipping quietly away with the afternoon sun. Finally, suspended there between Katherine's slender fingers, Polly's wrist, hand, and arm seemed to relax into the shape of an elegant swan.

While alive, Polly found it almost impossible to endure physical intimacy with her children. She was not a demonstrative person, nor did she often say, "I love you." But as the tumor in her brain began to grow, and as she became more physically impaired, she gradually changed. She allowed her children to feed her, to touch her, to kiss her. She told them repeatedly that she loved them; she forgot the barriers once constructed to protect her from such intimacy. And something like healing began to occur. While she was in her "right mind," she was never able to forgive herself for her perceived sins, nor was she able to accept the idea of God forgiving her. No matter how much I or anyone else tried to help, nothing seemed to lighten her burden. It was only when the disease process fully took over and death was but hours away that she became more vague but less tortured, more fragile but less brittle.

Now, completely undefended, her strength and beauty seeped to the surface. The tension in her forehead had been released, the tightness of her mouth and jaw relinquished. Her daughters moved through the apartment like temple priests, quietly, reverently. Taking turns, they would leave the room then circle back, touching the sacred stone from which they came. Their mother's last exhalation, the last particles of living breath that had circulated through her body, still lingered in the room. Polly was literally in the air that they were breathing. They were absorbing her into their cells, knitting the mystery of her into the fabric of their lives. Maybe they never truly knew their mother until this moment, until she had fully surrendered—to them, to the Divine, to the truth that it is only our illusion that keeps us from experiencing peace and joy. In death, Polly dropped her mask and revealed herself. And there, beneath the rubble of personality, of flesh and blood, of life experiences, was the spirit who had lived in the confines of their mother's body all along. Her daughters seemed to recognize this—they felt her love and were able to love her more fully in return.

I'd like to think that there was a flicker of a moment in which Polly was aware of this before she died. In that imperceptible pause between the last exhale and the extinguishing of consciousness, I would like to think that she was pleasantly surprised—startled even—by the love and forgiveness that was always there. If she had an "aha!" moment, however, she was keeping it to herself because her expression was as enigmatic as the face of a sphinx.

I pondered that last image of Polly for many months. I would see her in my mind, see the graceful *S* of her raised arm, the curved line flowing from her fingertips to her elbow, and wonder what it was that I was still struggling to learn from her. Maybe I was trying to unearth the primary cause of her suffering, as if in doing so, I could go back in time and be a better help to her. Or maybe it was her Mona Lisa face that continued to intrigue me. Did God come to her? Did she find peace? The clues to the answers to these questions seemed buried in the coded message of her surrendered arm.

What is it to surrender—to life, to love, to death, to mystery? All of these, in some way, are one and the same. They are part of a wheel that continues to spin, offering opportunities for spiritual growth, for new understanding, and for the experience of being connected to the Divine. Whether Polly's spirit transformed into her swan-self, I will never know—but her daughters were transformed. Witnessing this was miracle enough. It took me years to understand it, years to really see that it wasn't just Polly's story I was witnessing: it was the story of a family and of the generations to come. The swan was revealed not when Polly died, but rather when her daughter tenderly lifted her mother's hand to her lips. It was revealed in that simple act of love and acceptance, one that transcended the wounds of the past—the moment daughter cradled mother, mother became divine, and beauty emerged from the chrysalis of forgiveness.

Last Call

Sitting on the plane, I leaned my forehead against the window, my chin in my hand, and watched the ground crew do their work. Armed with illuminated orange sticks, they waved their signals and stood their ground before the giant winged beasts that were about to take flight. Night was falling across a stormy sky, and there was an occasional flash of lightning in the distance, as if someone was turning the lights off and on in another room. I had a front row seat across from the cabin door, where I could easily watch people making their way across the tarmac. It was a small plane and a small airport, one in which passengers had to walk outside to board their aircrafts. The wind was picking up, blowing summer skirts and lending an air of wildness and risk to the otherwise mundane process. Like herd animals, docile and obedient, everyone complied with directions. They walked quickly past the other planes, they stayed in line, they let the shepherds with the orange staffs guide them. From the security of my seat, I absentmindedly observed the passengers who were boarding—a young couple with two children, a few businessmen and women, a pair of college-aged girls—aware that we were about to become indiscernible cargo hurtling through the sky together, our fates entwined, at least for the next two hours.

I wasn't supposed to be on the plane. That fact alone was unnerving to me. The advent of September 11 had exacerbated and magnified my latent fear of flying. Even years later, too many gruesome images remained in my mind from working as a chaplain to the morgue at Ground Zero, and I was still haunted by the stories of chance and circumstance. Some people survived that terrible day because they had decided to take a day off or had taken a later train. Some were delayed in traffic or had stayed home with a sick child. The stories were endless. A man missed a flight, a woman stepped out to grab a coffee, and another lingered for an extra moment in the sunshine of that lovely morning—simple random acts that inexplicably saved their lives. On the other hand, some who weren't supposed to be at the World Trade Center or on a plane that day died. Some made last-minute plans to attend a meeting, or decided to admire the view from Windows on the World. Others just did what they did every weekday morning—kissed their children, left their homes, and headed to work. One could go crazy trying to understand the brutality of luck or destiny, depending on one's point of view. Those who are spared tragedy, those who have won the cosmic coin toss, are sometimes tempted to say, "Everything happens for a reason." For example, "the reason my tire blew that morning was to prevent me from dying," or "God must've kept me from getting on that plane." But for the bereft, the very idea of a divinely orchestrated fate is a slap in the face—a cruel luxury belonging to those who survive. Either way, we are left with an endless stream of *what-ifs?*

I tried not to play that game as I sat on the plane, but the combination of bad weather and strange circumstances let the horse out of the barn, so to speak. No amount of intellectualizing or praying could stop my mind from racing, and I was coming closer than I ever have to experiencing a panic attack. Rationally, I knew that I was making myself crazy, but I couldn't help it. My husband and children had left on an earlier flight, en route from New York to Duluth, Minnesota, for a cruise around the Great Lakes with extended family members. I looked out the window, picturing them somewhere in the vast ocean of sky with its rolling thunder and no guarantees. They were heading west, chasing the sun into what I hoped were clearer skies, sprinting ahead of this threatening storm. I shut my eyes for a moment, thinking of them all traveling together, and said a prayer.

What if I'm not supposed to be on this plane? Fear rumbled in my head, my own internal thunder causing my heart to beat a little faster. *Maybe I will perish because of this.* On the other hand, I argued, *What if I am supposed to be on this plane? Maybe I will be in Duluth to prevent a terrible thing from happening to one of the children. Maybe I will say, "I am so glad I heeded that nudge to come."* The idea that we are ultimately in charge of our destinies seems absurd when stacked up against all we cannot control, and yet we continue to try and outwit the Universe.

I had chosen to take a later flight for a variety of reasons, although the only one I could say out loud was because our cat had gone missing three days earlier. If you're an animal lover and know what it is like to consider a pet as part of the family, you'll know there was no way I was going to leave for eight days with Eli, our one-eyed cat, lost outside, maybe injured, dead, or stuck somewhere starving or dehydrating.

That reason was true, of course, but so was the reality that I had been ambivalent about the trip to begin with. The past nine months had been a nightmare. I was still putting myself back together after my bout with cancer, my brother had died, and a teenager who was like a daughter to me was dealing with a devastating illness that was wreaking havoc on her health and on her psyche. Her suffering was almost unbearable, for her first and foremost, for her family, and for me as her support and confidant. I wanted to absorb it, to take it from her, to soak it into my body so that I could rid her of the pain. I felt like a wild animal, frantic, howling, pacing, growling, trying to protect my young; she was the cub, trapped and terrified. She hurled her anguish at me and at those closest to her, as if this plague were somehow our fault, as if we had brought this upon her. Most of the time, she was aware that blaming others was irrational and unfair, but in the heat of the moment it didn't matter. What mattered was that it was happening, and I was utterly powerless to change the course of events for her, no matter how desperately I tried. It was like trying to push back a tornado with my bare hands.

As the trip approached, I was feeling spiritually and emotionally wrung out. My husband and I discussed the possibility of my staying home, using that week to rest and to recharge, to write and to reflect, but I couldn't imagine not being there for my children. They had suffered, too, during my time of emotional fatigue, and they were looking forward to being together. How *could* I stay home? The prospect seemed indulgent and selfish.

When Eli disappeared three days before we were to leave, I spent hours searching and calling, calling and searching—especially in the marsh behind our house—and I contemplated what this might mean in terms of the trip. I looked for a Bigger Reason. Did his escape happen to give me a graceful way to opt out of the trip? The part of me that reads into things, that tries to find meaning and guidance in the twists and turns that happen in life, thought maybe the answer was *yes.* Yes, I was supposed to stay home and repair my spirit. Yes, I was meant to have some respite from the anguish and the despair, the worry and the intensity surrounding issues of illness. Yes. The word was like an exhalation—and I'd been holding my breath for so long.

On the eve of our departure date, the third full day of Eli's escape, I was putting "Lost" flyers in mailboxes throughout the neighborhood. As I went about my work, I called Eli's name, without much hope of a reply. But suddenly, a small cry came in response to my calls. When I heard this, my heart leapt. I called again and followed the sound. At the edge of the marsh near my neighbor's house, I spotted a cat lounging in the sun on a nest of fallen stalks. Eli! Looking over his shoulder, appearing relaxed and uninjured, he blinked at me with that one good eye, making little mews as I called to him. But when I took a step closer, he scrambled to his feet and disappeared into the tall marsh grasses. "Eli!" I cried, a little too desperately, unable to keep my voice calm and reassuring. I dropped the flyers with his picture on them, sending them scattering into the marsh. As they tumbled away, they looked like old "Wanted" posters from the Wild West, featuring Eli, the one-eyed outlaw.

"Here kitty-kitty-kitty . . . ELI!" I tried to follow him but the marsh grasses were over eight feet tall, at the height of their life cycle, thick and unyielding. They felt alive, like strange thin guards barring my way and holding me back. I could not believe how impossible it was to follow Eli through those grasses. I flailed wildly against them but it was pointless: he was gone. I spent the next five hours sitting near the spot where I had seen him, calling his name and feeling alternately desperate and mad. At first, I could not believe that I had seen him; after several hours of sitting there, I could not believe he refused to come to me.

Spotting Eli threw another monkey wrench into the decision-making process for the trip. Not only was he alive, he was close by. Now it would be even harder for me to just leave without first getting him back inside. "He's probably really scared," I told my husband. "Maybe I can arrange a later flight tomorrow, which would give me just a little more time to get him in."

When my husband and children left our house the next morning before seven, my children's faces were a mixture of disbelief and desperation. "You *are* coming, aren't you, Mommy?" (I was still "Mommy" when they needed me and "Mom!" when they were mad at me.)

"Yes," I told them. "I'll be there. Promise."

I watched as their car disappeared down the road, then I went into the backyard and began calling for Eli. My neighbors' windows flanked my yard like nosy sentries; I glanced up at them, hoping no one would be too annoyed that I was doing this so early in the morning. But the only sound I heard was the whisper of the marsh grasses and the occasional crackle made by a falling twig.

The marsh was either haunted or alive. It snapped and rustled from places you could not see, holding its secrets behind a thick curtain that swayed hypnotically in the breeze. And the breeze seemed to be blowing relentlessly, shaking the tops of the reeds until they shimmered and waved like a thousand tiny hands, tamping down any sound that might be coming from below. Several times I thought I heard Eli creeping toward me. The underbrush would crunch—and then nothing. I would strain my ears, sucking the empty air for sound until I felt like I was drowning in silence or choking on a tidal wave of marsh grass. The ebb and flow of sound and silence took on a rhythm of its own. I sat still as a stone, the coyote in me sniffing the breeze, every cell on high alert. I would sense Eli near, then his presence would recede with the tide. When it rolled in again, it would carry only the song of a bird or the relentless rustle of the reeds.

As I sat at the edge of our back fence—that which kept the marsh at bay—listening and calling, I thought of my kids. If I decided to stay home, would they think I put an animal's needs before theirs, that Eli was more important than they were? I pictured them years from now on a cartoon therapist's couch: "It all started when I realized my mom loved her cat more than me . . ." I cringed at the thought. Then I began to get mad at Eli. His refusal to come out of the marsh began to feel like a conscious choice. He knew where home was; he could hear me calling him—why wasn't he coming?

At about ten, the phone rang. The family's flight to Duluth was delayed; an hour or so later it was canceled. This, of course, caused a mini traveling frenzy. Every passenger was scrambling for a seat on the next flight—or any flight—leaving New York in the right direction. My family was in the midst of that chaos, their plans now uncertain. *That's it*, I thought, *I'm not going. I'll never get a flight.* Just to be sure, I called the airline. To my surprise, the woman on the other end of the line not only rebooked me, but informed me that there would be no charge to change my ticket since my previously scheduled flight had been canceled. Suddenly I was thrust back into limbo. *OK. This really does mean that I am supposed to go. Eli, you will have to make do.*

I booked the flight, hung up the phone, and took a deep breath. Looking around, I realized how absolutely unprepared I was to go, how I had never really wanted to go, even before Eli slipped out. The house was quiet—a quiet that I would not experience now that I was going on this family cruise. It would be the first time in four years that we had taken a family vacation. I could say that this was because of money; I could say that it was because someone always had to stay home to take care of our menagerie of pets, or that my husband took the kids on vacations by himself so that I could write. It all made sense on the surface and was true to some degree, but it was not the heart of the matter. I stayed home because I needed space—space to think, to write, yes, but also space to try to figure out my life. Melancholy had taken over my soul like a fungus, like mold, deep green and slick and impossible to climb out of. Still, I went on, year after year, through cancer, through treatment, never making the internal shift that I thought my illness might inspire. I played the part of being OK, but the mold was beginning to climb the walls again. That was my fear, anyway.

I didn't spend a lot of time thinking about it as I ran around my house, writing lengthy instructions to the friend who had agreed to care for the animals, and cleaning. I put out food and water for Eli, knowing full well that the raccoons would get to them long before he would. I went through the motions, scanning the marsh every chance that I could. Any time I began to waver about leaving, I would think of my children's faces—both as they left and as I imagined they'd look when they saw me standing in Duluth. It was the right thing to do. I could do it. I *had* to do it. The kids needed me, and that had to take precedence over everything else.

I called my mother to let her know what was happening, but I already knew what she would say: I'd made the right choice. Her voice was soothing and reassuring on the other end of the phone. She knew how upset I was about Eli; she knew how hard it was for me to leave him . . . and yet . . . the priority had to be my family. *But what about me?* I wanted to say. *What about me? No one seems to notice that I am dying here.*

All of those thoughts were swirling in my head as I sat on the plane. Was I martyring myself by going on this trip? Yes, in some ways I knew I was. I was going not because I wanted to, but because I thought it was the right thing to do. Isn't that what parenting is about? Putting your children's needs above your own? Isn't it about sacrifice and protection and going to extremes because you love so ferociously? I felt all of those things without effort. But I also knew I wouldn't be good to anyone dead, or depressed, or only half-alive. I also had to attend to my own soul. Like the flight announcement goes: "If you are traveling with a small child, remember to place the oxygen mask over your own face first." I tended to hold the mask over everyone's nose but my own, and now I couldn't think clearly, deprived as I was of oxygen.

From seat 1B, I texted my best friend: I'm freaking out. Did I make a mistake? On plane ready to head twd Chicago. Help!

Her answer: No mistakes. All good. U made a loving choice. I love u

Me: I love u too! I'm a mess

Best Friend: Trust

Me: I will try to let go now. Trust will be my mantra

The flight attendant shut the cabin door. I turned off my phone and pulled out a folded piece of paper that I had retrieved from my daughter's room before I left for the airport. It contained a Sanskrit chant for protection and peace that my friend Jenny had given her in New Zealand. Cat had used it to calm her fears when flying so far alone, and she said that it had worked. It gave me comfort and courage to think of her saying the same words only a couple weeks before, on a plane traveling halfway around the world, and so I started chanting. I said the words out loud as rhythmically and earnestly as I could. I repeated and repeated them until I noticed my breathing had eased and my heart had stopped pounding. I was praying for guidance and protection, and it didn't matter what language I used. *It is all about faith and intention,* I thought.

It's a good thing I was in a better space when the captain made an announcement over the loudspeaker. "Ladies and gentlemen," he said in a calm, authoritative voice, "it looks like we are going to be delayed here for a while due to severe thunderstorms in Chicago. All flights have been suspended going in or out of the Chicago airports. I'm going to see if we can get clearance to let you step off the aircraft for a little while."

With that, the cabin door was opened once again. There was a whoosh of fresh, warm air. *Escape.* Could it be that I was being presented once more with a choice, an opportunity? Rain had begun to fall. The shepherds on the ground with their orange staffs pulled on hoods and hats; the wind billowed their jackets. After a few minutes, the captain's voice came over the intercom again, saying we could deplane, but instructing us to take our carry-ons with us and to stay near the gate area. I got to my feet, trying not to appear too anxious, and retrieved my small bag from the overhead compartment. I began to regret that I'd checked my luggage through to Duluth, but I tried not to dwell on this. After all, what did it matter? I was going to get back on that plane with the rest of the cattle, wasn't I?

When I stepped out of the cabin door and onto the metal ladder, I took a deep breath. The air was full of negative ions pumping energy and life into the night. Compared to the air on the plane, it was like stepping into pure oxygen. The ground crew waved me onward. I steadied myself because the steps were slick with rain, but I needed no prodding to hurry. There was nothing I wanted more than to descend those steps. The feeling of reprieve, of being given a second chance as my feet hit solid ground, is nearly impossible to describe.

As I ran inside the small terminal, the atmosphere was chaotic. It was filled with passengers awaiting flights that had been delayed and those who were just arriving—the human equivalent of a multicar pileup. A line had already begun to form at the ticket counter; clearly

I was not the only passenger in danger of missing my connection in Chicago. People, spattered with rain, were steadily emerging through the open door and streaming past me. I recognized some of my fellow passengers. The couple with the two small boys looked anxious as they tried to weigh their options; the college girls ran in laughing, undaunted. I stood in line, dreading my interaction with the gate agents, who had proven less than friendly when I had arrived at the airport several hours before. It had been so quiet then. I was the only one in line when I checked in, making me wonder where everyone else was. *If they were rude then,* I thought, *just imagine how they would be under pressure!* People were talking on cell phones, they were madly texting on their tiny keypads or opening their laptops. Everyone seemed to be vying for a place on the next flight, just in case.

I decided to step out of the line, avoiding the harried agents, and simply called the airline to see if I was going to miss my connection in Chicago. No surprise: I was. "The best I can do for you," said a cheery anonymous voice, "is to book you on the first flight out of Chicago in the morning. Unfortunately, it flies to Minneapolis, not Duluth. I'm afraid you'll have to figure out a way to get to your final destination."

"OK," I said with a small sigh of resignation. "Book me on that six-fifteen flight."

As I ended the call, my stomach lurched. I stared out the open terminal door. It looked like a dark hole, an abyss from which there would be no returning. I was afraid it would suck me from the terminal if I stood too close. Strange, how the night had looked warm and welcoming from the inside of the plane just moments before. But now everything was turned inside out. My heart began to pound again. I heard someone say that the people on the Delta flight, the plane that we had run past twice now, had been sitting on the tarmac for over two hours. I pictured the passengers within the plane, looking out at the terminal, out at the night, and wondered what they might be thinking. Although I felt a little guilty about this, I was glad not to be one of them.

My head was spinning and my mouth began to get dry. I could feel in my gut that the chances of getting out of Chicago in the morning in time to make that boat launch in Duluth were very slim. How much did I want to go on this trip? How committed was I and how hard was I willing to try? At this point, I assumed my family was already in the air and on their way. I called my husband, just in case, but the call went right to voicemail. Not knowing what else to do, I texted another friend and told her about the delay. *Oh no! Just stay in a good space,* she texted back. Ignoring her advice, I called my mother.

"Mom, I am freaking out here. The weather is terrible, and I'm really afraid, and I know I'm gonna miss my connection, and even if I get there, I doubt if I can make it out of Chicago in the morning in time for the boat! The night looks like death to me, and my heart is pounding. I'm sorry to call you like this, but I wanted you to know."

Her voice was light and steady. She told me to just get on the plane and go to Chicago. She assured me that the pilot would not fly if he felt it was too dangerous, and she promised me that I would not crash. "But then again," she said, laughing, "I'm not a white-knuckle flier like your father! I just figure, if it's time to go, it's time to go. Not that *you* should think that, because you're younger and those children need you, but I trust the pilot's judgments. Just go ahead and get on. You can figure out what to do once you're in Chicago."

"Mom!" I cried. "Don't tell me to get on! If something happens to me, you'll feel terrible. I know you—you would feel responsible, like you had pushed me to go. I shouldn't have called you!" At this, my mother started laughing again. For some reason, she found it very funny that I was thinking more about her feeling bad than about me dying in a plane crash.

Then Mom (still laughing) said, "Your father is screaming at me to tell you to *stay off that plane!* He doesn't want you to reboard. But, like I said, he's a white-knuckle flier! I know he would be doing the same thing that you are; there's no way he'd get back on. He'd just try again in the morning."

I told her I loved her and that I would let her know right away what I decided to do. Something about our conversation made me want to go even less. Martyrdom. It was the feeling that I should do this for everyone else: for my children, for my father-in-law (who had paid for the trip), for appearances to prove what a good person and good mother I was. "I really think the children need you," my mother said before hanging up, "but do what you need to do."

The announcement to reboard the plane came over the garbled PA system. Our time on the ground had somehow evaporated. It was as if the minutes had been sucked into that black hole just outside the door. There was still a long line of worried, impatient, or irritated passengers at the ticket counter, but the agents were ignoring them, focused now on shuffling us out of the terminal, out of their hair, and on our merry ways. People around me gathered their bags and scrambled to their feet, walking quickly out the door where they broke into trots as the rain spattered them like buckshot. The couple with the children looked at each other, shrugged, and each took the hand of the nearest child. Though burdened with backpacks and juice boxes, books and teddy bears, they moved with remarkable precision. At once lumbering and efficient, they kept glancing around in case they were forgetting something. *I remember those days,* I thought. *The plane couldn't possibly crash with those little boys on board, could it?* I was clearly out of my mind.

"Last call!" shouted the ticket agent. "All remaining passengers must board at this time." I took a few steps toward the agent in the tight blue uniform, who looked like she wanted to rip my head off. I peered out at the night with its swirling, foreboding darkness. There was not a drop of moisture in my mouth. My heart was in my throat; it was pulsing in my face; it was squirting out my ears. "Are you boarding or not?" barked the agent without trying to conceal her impatience. For another moment, I stood frozen. And then something within me said, *Choose life.*

"No," I said, with my Sahara-dry mouth. "No. I'm not getting back on."

"You're not flying." (More of a statement than a question.)

"No."

Without another glance at me, she put a walkie-talkie to her lips and gave the all clear. "Wait! What about my bag?" I asked.

"Too late," came the disinterested reply. My bag would go off without me—on to Chicago, on to Duluth—and my seat would remain empty. The door to the black hole of death closed and sealed in front of me. I had finally made the choice to stay home.

For a few minutes, I stood there blinking under the fluorescent lights, unsure of what to do next. The terminal had emptied around me, as if everyone had been swept out with the tide, out via the sinkhole. Both awed and horrified by my own actions, I sank into a chair and tried to reason with myself. Hadn't the Universe given me numerous chances to stay home? Hadn't I ignored those signals because I was trying to do the "right thing"? And then, when presented with this last unexpected opportunity, hadn't something from deep within said *live*? And living meant taking care of myself for once. Whatever spark still burned, whatever part of me still yearned to live, *that* part said, *Everyone will be fine. You need to rest. You need to heal.*

In retrospect, I don't think that I truly believed the plane would crash, not deep down, although those fears were certainly screaming on the surface. I was afraid that *I* would crash. I had come to a crossroad with no guarantees, no signposts—only the compass in my gut.

I called my husband to tell him what had happened and was surprised when he answered. They had been delayed once again. I started to cry; he was soothing and reassuring; he would make the kids understand. I told him I might try again to catch a flight in the morning, but I didn't really believe this—nor did he.

An hour later, I was in my bed, surrounded by the familiar quiet, by the unseen ghosts who roam my house, by my dogs and my one remaining cat. I exhaled deeply, squeezing out the used-up oxygen in my lungs and the toxins released by my fear. I breathed out the stale air of the airport and the haughty venom of the agents. I let go of my indecision, my guilt, and my shame. And I breathed in the peace that I had finally chosen in the flash of a moment, on the precipice of despair.

In the end, the plane bound for Chicago landed safely. There were no screaming headlines in the morning alerting the nation to a tragedy. The college girls would have a story to tell; the weary young parents would kiss their children good morning. The boat would pull out of Duluth's harbor with a ceremonial blast of its horn, and my children would start an adventure filled with beauty and laughter. Was there divine guidance in my decision making? If so, had I listened? I revisited each twist in the road, looking for a sign I might have missed and feeling slightly embarrassed about my panic attack.

Sometimes God's hands are like the illuminated orange cones of the ground crew, clearly waving *This way! This way!* And sometimes God's voice comes over a loudspeaker, saying, *Last call to board!* And sometimes God appears in the wild frenzy of a storm, reminding us that we are powerless over the unknown and all we cannot control. What does not waver, however, is that we are loved. Living or dying, stumbling or shining, we are loved. Perhaps this was the lesson for me. Perhaps it really didn't matter what I chose to do or how it would turn out; what mattered was discovering and surrendering to the deep awareness of God's abiding presence. God was in the grouchy flight attendants as much as in the laughing college girls; God was in the raging storm as much as in the starry expanse that sparkled above the clouds. God was in my choice to stay home as much as in my urge to be with my family. If I could see God in everything, then I could understand myself as a brushstroke, a single note in an eternal symphony, whose one breath is om.

It is hard to remember this when we are faced with a difficult choice, with a crisis, with heartache, or with any of the myriad problems that come with being human, but that is the challenge of faith. The life that we know on earth is a cosmic crucible for spiritual growth. How we live is important, for we learn how to synchronize our souls with the Divine, but how we interpret the things that happen to us fortifies our courage and gives us strength for the journey.

As for Eli, he appeared on the front porch just after midnight the night before my family's return. He'd been gone for twelve days but returned looking no worse for the wear. His coat was glossy; he appeared well fed. The only signs of his adventure were the scratches on my arms, incurred as I struggled to get him inside. Squirming and flailing wildly, he nearly escaped again, but once inside, it was as if he had never left. Later that night, he sat on my chest, purring loudly and luxuriating in the safety of the familiar. As I rubbed his head, he looked at me with that one green eye. What he knows, I will never know, and what moves him I may never feel. But staring into his crooked poker face, his Cheshire grin, I sensed that we were on the same side. We were sharing a hand with all its terrible unknowns and its unexpected miracles, left to interpret for ourselves what is real, what is chance, what is meant to be, and how we are to play the cards that we are dealt.

The Resonance of Lavender

Driving to Mount Sinai Hospital in New York City for my annual World Trade Center health check always dredges up something of what it felt like to report to Ground Zero for a shift. I suppose that's understandable: the only reason I go to Mount Sinai each year is because of my work as a chaplain to the morgue at Ground Zero during the year of recovery after the September 11 attacks. The World Trade Center Health Program, set up to monitor and treat 9/11-related health conditions, hopes to catch any additional cancers or illnesses early, but the annual checkup is a double-edged sword: it nudges me to take care of my health while reminding me of the ever-present possibility of illness due to exposure at Ground Zero.

This year, as in years past, I drive to the city alone. I know which garage to park in now, which hospital entrance is the correct one, and which elevator to take. I no longer feel lost in the cavernous lobby of the hospital, where a sea of doctors and nurses move purposefully about and voices echo off the high ceiling. I just walk in a preprogrammed kind of way, neither hesitating nor hurrying. I know that the waiting room will be packed when I reach the right floor, and there will be papers to sign, and other people who are also waiting for their names to be called.

After signing in at the reception desk, I find a seat facing the television. The news is playing with the sound muted; words scroll across the bottom in a never-ending river. I glance around the room, wondering with mild curiosity if I might recognize anyone from my time at Ground Zero. I haven't yet. Like the television in the corner, my mind is filled with silent images. Some are from my time spent at the Trade Center fifteen years ago; these bump up against the current images of the men and women around me. I wonder who might have been a fireman or a cop, a construction worker or a volunteer. It occurs to me that we are all getting older. If we make eye contact with one another we usually smile, in a somber kind of way. It's as if the edges of the mouth go up while the eyes sink. That look is what connects us.

I get through the usual series of tests. The only part that is a routine stress for me is having my blood drawn. Because of my cancer diagnosis years ago, the technician can use only my right arm. But those veins are shot—too many punctures from infusions and surgeries make the task of drawing blood difficult. Try as I might not to stress out, my heart pounds when I extend my arm for the technician. He is kind and thoughtful as he taps various places on my hand, arm, and wrist. I look away after he chooses his spot, making every effort to breathe deeply. When the task is finished, I feel as if I might pass out, and tell him so. Embarrassed, I try to explain about the infusions and the trauma to my veins. He nods understandingly, tells me to put my head down, and then brings me a glass of water.

When I've completed the circuit of tests and examinations, which takes about three hours, I head back down to the lobby. Again I feel the ghost tingles of Ground Zero. As it was after nearly every shift, one part of me is glad to be done and another is reluctant to leave. It's strange. I find myself lingering in the lobby for a moment. The bustle of professionals and visitors is reassuring somehow, a reminder that life goes on. I remind myself that this is where my son was born, nearly six years before the attacks; thus, it is a place of life, as well as a reminder of death for me.

I'm heading toward the door when I notice a woman standing behind a small table. The sign hanging from it reads, *Blessing of the*

Hands, Sponsored by the Department of Spiritual Care. I am familiar with this practice from my own hospital work. The idea is to offer a blessing to anyone who might be interested, by anointing their hands with a drop of oil. I am usually the one offering the blessing, so I am curious about what it means to be on the other side of the table. I observe the woman behind the table as people bustle past, seemingly oblivious to her and to what she is offering. No one is stopping. I start down the stairs toward the door, then I turn around and head back toward her. *What the heck,* I think to myself. *I could use a blessing.*

The woman, who is slightly older than myself, and who wears no particular religious identification, smiles as I approach. She is one of the chaplains at the hospital. She asks me if I have a religious affiliation, which will guide her as she prays. I appreciate her sensitivity, and confess that I am a Methodist and a hospice chaplain. Without intending to, I also tell her that I have just finished my annual World Trade Center health exam.

"That was hard work," she says quietly as she looks, unflinchingly, into my eyes. Taking my hands in hers, palms up, she places a drop of lavender oil on each wrist. Then she tells me to rub them together. The lovely aroma of the oil reaches my nose. Calm seeps in through my pores, and I feel myself beginning to let go of the stress of the exam. With head bowed, she begins to pray with her face close to mine. Her accent is musical and rich, *Jamaican,* I think. I do not try to figure it out; I just let her words flow over and around me like the gentle lapping of waves. For a moment, she is the ocean and I am the beach, and she is calling me back to herself, reclaiming me and reminding me of my Source.

With this blessing and the lingering fragrance of lavender, I return to my car. Now I am ready to go home. Lost in thought, I head north on Madison Avenue toward the RFK Triborough Bridge that will take me back to Westchester. After driving for a few minutes, I realize that I have missed my usual turn toward the bridge, forcing me to snake my way through local city traffic. I'm not bothered, particularly, because I'm in no hurry and am in a peaceful place. As I slow to a stop at a traffic light, I notice a man standing outside of the car in front of me: a panhandler asking for money. Unlike in years past, these days it is fairly unusual to have people tapping on your car window in New York City. The local government and NYPD have effectively cracked down on the practice. My first thought is a reflexive *Oh no* even as I reach over for my wallet to fish out some money.

I am pulling a five-dollar bill out of its otherwise empty compartment when I glance up at the man who has reached my passenger window. Dressed in a faded green army jacket, he looks to be in his late sixties. The stubble of a beard covers his weathered face, and his eyes have a milky quality, as if the brown of his irises has begun to melt from floating too long there. The traffic light is still red, giving me enough time to roll down my window and stretch over to pass him the money. As I do, he holds up his hands with a sad smile. He has no fingers or thumbs on either hand. Instead, there are only crevices, indentations, between which he manages to clasp the bill. "Thank you so much," he says. "God bless you." The light turns green and I continue on my way, conscious that I have received two blessings today. And I wonder: If I hadn't been open to the first, would I have missed the second?

Blessing of the Hands is what the sign at the hospital read. When the chaplain blessed my hands, did she open them as well? And with my hands, my heart? Without that blessing, I might have missed the stranger with no fingers, and thus the opportunity to touch the hands of God, to be blessed by the incognito Christ. "I am the least of these," Jesus tells us. "I am the sick and the poor, the hungry and the naked." Time and again, we miss the opportunities we have in our lives to touch God's hands—and they are often bruised and dirty. They don't always look like ours. They are often not our same color or faith. They are not confined to the hands we hold at the dinner table or at church; they are the hands that knock on our car windows or reach to us from the sidewalk.

Sitting at the traffic light, the imperative to give seemed pretty simple. What I received, however, was anything but. Receiving a blessing is not like receiving a gift; it's more than that. It's a commission. If we don't allow it to move through us like purifying water, extending out to others, we become bloated. If we don't open ourselves to receive it in the first place, our hearts become parched and brittle. Looking back at that day, I realize just how many blessings I received, how many opportunities I'd been given to feel the presence of God. In the knowing eyes of the others in the waiting room, I found company; in the gentle compassion of the lab tech, I found comfort; in the prayer of the chaplain, I found healing. My heart was so full by the time I reached the stranger at the red light that I not only welcomed the opportunity to give, I needed it. And so it was that I had fingers; this man had none. I had money; this man had none. I had the resonance of lavender—but he had the benediction.

Knocking on Heaven's Door

Sitting on the gurney in my thin green hospital gown, I was about as relaxed as one could be just prior to surgery. This was not my first rodeo—in fact, it was my sixth. Sixth breast surgery that is, this one being the second in a series of outpatient procedures aimed at replacing the implant in my mastectomy breast with my own tissue. It sounded like a win-win situation, a "two-fer," the doctor had joked. I would get the uncomfortable implant out, while fat from another part of my body would be happily welcomed into its new home in my breast. The first procedure, albeit more than I'd bargained for, had gone well. The second was moving me closer to the possibility of putting this whole nasty business of cancer behind me. Having my own tissue, a warm breast for the first time in years, thinner thighs . . . who could argue with that? I was ready to go.

Before turning off my phone, I indulged in a quick selfie, complete with a cheesy thumbs-up, and sent it to my friends and family. *Looking forward to a little snooze,* I joked.

Geez, some girls will do anything just to get some rest, someone answered. I smiled, knowing that I would be free of worry, pain, and conscious thought for a few hours. I wasn't looking forward to the recovery process, but I had no qualms about going under.

The surgical nurse came in to place my IV and have me sign a few last papers. I recognized him from the first of these procedures, which

I'd had twelve weeks before. I was relieved when I saw him because he was skilled at placing the IV, and his presence put me at ease. Next came the nurse anesthetist, a young man I'd never met. As he busied himself with the necessary preparations, I asked where the anesthesiologist was, the doctor who had taken care of me during my first surgery at the breast center. The nurse shrugged nonchalantly and said that he would be "starting" me and that Dr. P would "finish" me (in other words, bring me out of sedation). Whether it was his tone or the image of someone "finishing" me, I started to feel anxious.

"No offense," I said, "but I'd really like to see Dr. P before I go under. I woke up in pain last time and I'd like to talk to him. And, to be honest, I've never had a nurse put me under without a doctor present." At this, he proceeded to assure me about his training, bragging that he understood "even the tiniest bubble" in my IV. Then, despite my protests, he began to wheel me toward surgery, with the surgical nurse in tow.

When I said, again, that I would like to see the doctor (who, by the way, had given me something the last time to relax me prior to leaving the prep room, so that I didn't even remember being wheeled into surgery), the nurse responded with an irritated "Fine!" Stopping the gurney in the hallway, he began to push something through my IV, barely pausing before he continued rolling me toward the operating room. Almost immediately, I felt something like hot molten lava traveling up my arm and through my veins. It felt thick and heavy, scorching and excruciating.

"My arm is burning!" I cried. "It's on fire!"

"That's normal," he stated flatly, with hardly a glance in my direction.

"But I've never had that reaction before," I pleaded.

Then my head started swimming and my vision began to blur. "She's going," I heard the nurse say. But I wasn't going. Something terrible was happening. Cement was starting to take the place of my blood.

It was filling my limbs and traveling like a suffocating mudslide toward my lungs. In a moment, I knew it would overtake me.

"I can't breathe!" I gasped, reaching for my throat and giving one desperate kick of my leg in a futile attempt to get their attention. And then . . . I was paralyzed. Completely. Not just my limbs, but every part of me—my lungs, my face. I was completely frozen in my body: entombed. I couldn't move an eyelash, a nostril. I couldn't part my lips to take the tiniest sip of air. I could not make the slightest whimper of a cry to let anyone know that I was fully conscious but slowly suffocating. It was like being in a horror movie or the worst nightmare you could imagine. "At least we know we can put her out easily," joked the nurse anesthetist. *I'm not out,* I screamed silently, panic overwhelming me. *I'm not out; I'm suffocating. Can't you see I'm not breathing?*

They continued to wheel me toward surgery. I could feel the gurney moving and could see the light changing from behind my closed lids. I was dumbfounded that no one had noticed that I was suffocating. *Turn around!* I pleaded in my mind. *Just take a look at me!* Time had stopped but my thoughts were coming in rapid succession. I was screaming now in my head. *Help me! Somebody help me!* When it was clear that no one was responding, the words *What a stupid way to die* flashed in my mind. *Stupid and unnecessary,* I thought. *In fact, almost embarrassing. I never imagined my story would end this way.* I went from panic to anger to disbelief to sadness that my little life was coming to an end. All the while, the two male nurses chatted casually as they wheeled my dying body down the hall.

Then a strange thing happened: I started to let go. It was an active decision and one that, oddly, may have helped me preserve oxygen and save my own life. *If I am going to die,* I thought, *then I do not want my last thoughts to be ones of panic. I want to go calmly and willingly. I want to surrender peacefully.* And so I began to relax. The faces of my children flashed briefly in my mind's eye. *They still need me,* cried my heart, but I knew there was nothing I could do about this. All I could do was pray:

They will have to be OK. I will watch over you; I will come to you if I can. God, take care of them.

I became aware of all the many encounters I've had with death as a hospice chaplain. *Now I will finally get to see for myself,* I thought. *I will finally get to peek behind the curtain.* With this, I became spiritually curious. I strained my inner eyes to see what might be ahead—a crack of light, perhaps, or an opening behind which the Great Beyond could be revealed. I felt myself getting closer. Just in front of me was a panel of light, like a sliding, glowing door whose edges were ablaze. I was almost there, and I felt my spirits lighten.

I was so close now. The panel was about to slide open, revealing people on the other side. I was very sure of it, could feel the joy of it. I was reaching for it. Then, quite unexpectedly, I became acutely aware of my father's presence. My dad had been gone for a year and a half. He had been my spiritual mentor and friend, one with whom I had had endless animated conversations, from the earliest time I could remember, about life, death, and the spiritual realm. Dad! I could feel him at my right side. I knew, without a doubt, I would see him standing there in spirit form, if I could only open my eyes. He was that close. His hand was within reach. *I'll see you soon, Dad,* I said from the depths of me. If my face had not been frozen, I would have been smiling.

As soon as those words, *I'll see you soon,* leapt from my heart, I heard the surgical nurse yell, "Oh my God, look what's happening!" He noticed, finally, that I was not breathing and was in dangerous distress. Quite likely, I was turning blue. Although a faraway part of me registered relief, hearing his voice rattled me. I felt myself falling back into the body, the one that was made of cement. The panel of light began to recede—but my father's presence was still strong. The nurse anesthetist responded in a hushed but frantic, "OK, OK!"

He must have released the top of the gurney like a trap door, because my head was sent swinging like a heavy ball from the limp rope of my neck. He began pumping air into my mouth with some sort of handheld contraption. Although I was still unable to open my eyes, I could hear the rapid squeeze of the bag. And then, a silver thread of oxygen trickled down my throat. That's what it felt like: a thread as thin and strong as spider's silk being lowered into my throat and lungs. Instinctively, I reached for it. Oxygen! The tiniest sip. My spirit-self grabbed ahold of it, allowing it to carry me away from the threshold of light. I could still feel my father but his hand was slipping from mine. *It's not time* is what I felt him tell me. The anesthetist stopped pumping oxygen into me and instead shut my mouth tightly, which sent me into a tailspin. *Why are you doing that?* I thought. *Why are you stopping?* I felt like I was being tortured. Again, he dropped my head back and gave me a few more intense pumps of air before shutting my mouth. This time, he caught my bottom lip in my teeth. I felt searing pain, pain I was unable to convey, and the panic set in again. *Oh my God! He's going to put my teeth through my lip and he doesn't even know it, and there's nothing I can do.* Thankfully, he released my jaw, sending my head flopping back down again. That's the last thing I remember before waking up from surgery.

It turns out that the self-assured nurse anesthetist had mixed up the order in which my medications were to be administered. He mistakenly gave me the paralyzing agent first, a drug normally administered just prior to intubation, instead of the light sedation used to relax the patient. In other words, instead of feeling relaxed and sleepy, I was completely alert but paralyzed. What's more, his vigorous (and probably panicked) pumping of the manual ventilation bag caused my lung to collapse. It could have been worse, I later learned. This could have killed me. From what I understand, the nurses neglected to tell the doctor what had just happened, allowing him to go ahead and operate on me. When I woke up from surgery, I was gasping, *You almost killed me! I was suffocating!* Little did they know that I remembered everything that had happened prior to passing out. But I couldn't say very much because of my collapsed lung, and I was rushed from the outpatient facility to a hospital, where a chest tube had to be inserted.

There are many layers to this story, feelings and fears that I still have and am still processing, but it is the experience of the spiritual that I find most compelling. Clearly, I have thought a lot about death over the past twenty years. Because of my work, I have had the privilege of accompanying countless souls on their journeys toward whatever awaits us. I would like to think that I have helped walk them to the door, knowing that other hands, loving hands, are there to help them cross over. Now, that "door" has an image, as well as a feeling, attached for me. I return to it in my mind—the glowing panel, the sense of presence, and the feeling of wonder and acceptance. I would not have chosen to die at that moment but, if given no other choice, I was not afraid. The approaching transition from this life to the next was not scary; it was fascinating and peaceful. Having glimpsed this has been a comfort, both to me and to the families with whom I work. More than ever, I am confident that the person who is dying will feel the magnetic pull of unimaginable beauty and joy. Picturing loved ones floating freely toward the Divine, and toward those waiting to greet them, eases the pain of parting.

As I thought about what happened, I found it curious that I did not call out to God or even to Jesus when I was most terrified. Then I realized: I didn't need to call for God because God was the very plasma in which I was floating. I was a molecule of the Divine among a sea of others. Once I stopped struggling and surrendered to the current, I was not afraid. It was when I let go of my fear that I sensed my dad. His presence was a beautiful surprise, like the sudden appearance of a rainbow. I didn't have to conjure him, and I didn't have to see him; he was simply there with me. What I've come to understand is that I was enveloped in the Divine but still tethered to my humanness. And this part of me must have needed a tangible manifestation of love, and presence. I believe that's why my father came to me, why he was probably sent to me. The comfort of his familiar presence allowed me to reach for his hand, which meant I was, in essence, reaching for the hand of God. We are all stand-ins for the Divine—expressions of God's love—whether we manifest this or not, whether we try to bury our lights or let them shine. We cannot alter our divine nature, our spiritual DNA.

I'm glad that I have more time on this planet. I'm grateful that my children are not grieving the loss of their mother. I treasure the brush I had with my dad. But whenever my time comes to depart, I know there is something beyond this life, and I will be drawn to it like a baby to its mother's heartbeat. As created beings, we have a destiny and we have a destination. We are the rain that falls and becomes one with the ocean, and we are the invisible molecules that are absorbed back into the sky. In the circular flow to and from the Divine, we are never alone and we need not be afraid. We will always have each other—in this life and in the life to come.

The Choice

December 27, 2001. New York City is alive with holiday bustle. Sidewalks are packed with people, windows are decorated, families mill about. Everyone seems stubbornly determined to normalize this strange and terrible time. I find this both reassuring and disturbing. It's been three months since everything changed, and yet life goes on, dragging some of us along like tin cans tied to the back of a car. That's what I feel like in this mosh pit of post-Christmas shoppers and Ground Zero gawkers—a banged-up, invisible noisemaker, whose sound only I can hear. It's nobody's fault: not the young couple with the camera, not the father who hoists a child onto his shoulders, not the guy selling pictures of the Trade Center. The problem is that the world in which they exist no longer exists for me. Nothing is real until I cross the security checkpoint at Ground Zero. Then I can breathe. Then I feel that I belong in the picture.

The familiar rumble of trucks and the grind of machinery replace the noise of those outside the secured perimeter. The smell of roasting chestnuts mixes with the taste of wet cement in my mouth; soon this will be replaced by the unmistakable stench of decay. It's a strange thing to walk toward death—not your own, but that of others. What's stranger still is that this is the only place I feel fully alive. This is one of the unspoken secrets about working at Ground Zero. People are weary but alive. Workers are angry but not hateful. Friends and colleagues are devastated but not defeated. I see this in the eyes of the firefighters and in the tight jaws of the cops. Then again, it's been only three months. Perhaps bone-weariness has not yet set in; perhaps the heart hasn't yet fully broken—or maybe Ground Zero has become an island unto itself, whose inhabitants speak a secret language. Here, stories are told without fear of judgment or well-meaning-but-unwelcomed comments. Words do not have to be chosen carefully to avoid upsetting the listener. No one flinches or turns away. We are not required to integrate into a world that expects us to be who we were before. Beyond the perimeter is normalcy and people going on with their lives. Beyond the gates are also the grieving and the courageous, the survivors and the compassion of a nation. When I feel reluctant to leave the island at the end of a shift, I do so for all of those who never had that choice, those whose broken bodies I will bless, whose ashes I will carry with me on my shoes and in my lungs.

I'm here as a chaplain to the temporary morgue, or T-Mort, as it is commonly known. It is a sparse rectangular trailer, where bodies and pieces of bodies are brought as they are discovered. It is the first stop, the weigh station, on the long road home for those who were lost. Here, remains are documented, photographed, blessed. The blessing is my job, as it was for the chaplain whose shift I followed and as it will be for the one to follow me. We work in eight-hour rotations, forming a continual prayer wheel, one that turns and turns twenty-four hours a day. We are interchangeable; we are inter-religious. We light a flickering candle in this darkness to remind ourselves and others that meaning still exists and that God has not forgotten us. And when despair extinguishes that candle, as it routinely does, we do our best to light it again in defiant hope.

We have all chosen to be here—the chaplains, the firefighters, the EMTs, the police, the construction workers. That reality alone ties us to one another. Everyone has their own reasons. There is the fireman who was off duty that day but whose brother was not. When the towers fell, he promised his mother that he would not leave until he had found him. After two weeks of searching, he found a leg that bore his brother's familiar tattoo. A leg. That's what he could offer his mother when he finally came home—that and the fulfillment of his promise. There is the cop who has worked six days a week on the same corner of the site since it happened. When he goes home, the images that he has managed to hold at bay emerge to haunt his dreams. Only at Ground Zero does his heart return to its normal beat. Here, he does not have time to dwell on what he has seen. When this job is done, if it is ever done, he knows the ghosts will be waiting.

My choice to be here, not just at Ground Zero but also at the morgue, is something I never questioned. The moment the towers fell, my heart was already here. Two weeks later, when an Episcopal bishop asked me to take his shift for the night, the rest of me followed. I, like many clergy, wanted to help. And I suppose I felt more quali- fied than some because I was so well acquainted with death through my work as a hospice chaplain. To be part of the effort—to be able to *do* something—outweighed any forethought. It was like running into a dark forest in search of a lost child. In the heat of the moment, you don't think about the bears or the wolves. Once you're there, the enormity of the task, and the dread of what might be discovered, and the possibility of getting lost yourself, and the hopelessness that lurks in the shadows begin to press in.

The first time the bishop sent me to Ground Zero was for a mid- night to 8:00 a.m. shift. Under normal circumstances, especially at that hour, I could have made the drive from my suburb north of New York City in about thirty-five minutes. That night, however, I knew the roads would be closed at some point before I reached the site, and I wasn't even sure how close I could get via the subway. Jumping into the car had been like jumping off a cliff with my eyes shut. I threw myself in the right direction without knowing how or where I would land.

I remember how quiet my street was when I pulled out of the driveway. In the rearview mirror, all the houses looked like giant cribs, lined up in an orderly row, every inhabitant safely tucked in. The stability and the solidity felt comforting: everything and everyone would be here when I came home. I imagined running my hand lightly along every house, like a kiss good night or a blessing. Instead I whispered, "See you in the morning," and turned onto the highway.

Then my focus turned to what was ahead of me. I was anxious about how I would get there and whether I would have trouble passing through security. I was also unsure about what my work would entail, but I couldn't yet imagine, much less worry about, the possible risks or the long-term consequences. I was just hurling myself into the woods in search of something that had been lost, even though I wasn't sure what that was. I drove as far south as I could go on the FDR Drive before hitting the roadblocks; then I ditched my car in a twenty-four-hour parking garage and found a subway station.

When I descended the stairs and passed through the turnstile, the station was eerily quiet. My steps echoed loudly against the concrete, the sound bouncing off the dingy walls broadcasting my arrival. I became hyperaware of the fact that I was entirely alone at midnight in a deserted subway station somewhere under Lower Manhattan. The reality of being underground made my mouth go dry and my heart pound. Images of the towers falling and thousands of people being plunged and crushed into the ground were permanently carved in my mind. We had all seen them over and over and over again. The horror was so fresh. I could feel the blood starting to pulse in my ears. At that moment, I wasn't sure what I was more afraid of: being mugged or being buried under concrete by another attack. Either seemed imminently possible.

To my relief, two beams of light finally appeared from deep within the tunnel, quickly followed by the train that was pushing those headlights along. While I was glad to find that I wasn't the only one on the train, its riders were sparse. On any given night before September 11, things would have been different. People would have been gearing up for the night, happily talking over the music of the subway buskers. Parts of New York didn't really wake up until after midnight. If even New Yorkers were staying aboveground for the time being, then what was I doing under?

I rode as far as the train would take me. Emerging from the station a few blocks from Ground Zero, I felt strangely disoriented. Gone were the towers that functioned like the North Star for this part of the city. Now there was just a gaping hole in the inky black sky. As I tried to get my bearings, I was relieved to see St. Paul's Chapel in front of me, and a fair number of people walking around. The atmosphere of communal solidarity and scrappy tenacity was reassuring somehow.

I got through security without a problem (thanks to the bishop). Fire trucks lined the perimeter of the cordoned-off site; men waited their turn to pass buckets of debris from the pile. The frustration level was at a constant simmer. The wreckage in the center was a smoldering mountain of unfathomable proportions. The possibility of finding someone alive remained in the air, but it was as thin as a Communion wafer—as soon as you tasted it, it would dissolve in your mouth. And all that remained was the memory of that hope and the hunger for another taste.

For the next eight hours, I would walk and listen, listen and walk, offering comfort where I could. Spiritual support was not yet well organized, nor did we know what to hope or pray for. Initially, the Episcopal Church took the lead role in scheduling chaplains. In the immediate aftermath of the attacks, St. Paul's had opened its doors as a respite center, where hundreds of volunteers worked round the clock, serving food, handing out supplies, and offering support to those working at Ground Zero. It was, in itself, an overwhelming task. Unauthorized people were sneaking through security checkpoints by claiming to be chaplains. Some of them were motivated by curiosity, others by the opportunity to proselytize. On more than one occasion, I came upon someone pointing to the burning pile and telling any worker within earshot that they were headed for hell if they did not accept Jesus as their savior—or worse, someone condemning those who had surely died in the attack without being saved. This needed to be stopped, and the best way to do that was through tighter organization.

In November, the Red Cross took over the responsibility of vetting and assigning chaplains for work at Ground Zero. Interested clergy of all traditions were invited to meet at the office of the Episcopal Diocese of New York if we wanted to continue to volunteer. The Red Cross delineated several work areas, giving chaplains a choice about where we felt called to serve—the family centers, St. Paul's Chapel, the Marriott, the permanent or temporary morgues. There was no doubt in my mind where I belonged. *I have seen more dead bodies than most,* I reasoned, raising my hand for service at the morgue on site. I just never imagined that it would be body parts, and not bodies, that I would be blessing.

Since my first shift, the large black body bags have mostly been replaced by little red plastic ones, sometimes containing no more than a tooth or a piece of human tissue. The pile that burned for one hundred days is becoming an increasingly neat pit, hellfire preachers have been weeded out, and hope has given way to resolve. Around the perimeter, holiday lights glow from store windows, reminding us that life is ongoing, even when saturated by death. The dark and freezing night offers relief from the painful beauty of that September day—and every subsequent blue sky that has pierced me like a dagger. And so I welcome the white of winter. It's as if the color has been drained from the sky to help us start over.

I tuck my chin against the icy air as I walk. *The cold will help preserve the bodies,* I think. That's how it is with me these days. Everything is in relation to the Trade Center, to the bodies, and to the men and women working there. I take one more glance at the families shuffling along the sidewalk and feel a pang for my own children. An hour ago, I kissed them good night, but now they feel a world away. "Do you have to go again, Mommy?" my eight-year-old daughter asked from the warmth of her bed. My six-year-old son was already asleep. "I worry when you're gone, and it's still Christmas, and what if something happens to you?" Her eyes searched my face, revealing a too-grown-up awareness of life's precariousness. *What am I doing? What am I trying to prove?* I often asked myself these questions—until I walked onto the site. That's when the conflict and the self-reproach stopped. I can't imagine I was alone in this feeling.

My daughter is strangely accustomed to the idea of death, not just because of September 11 but also because it is a frequent topic of conversation in our house. Growing up with a mother who is a hospice chaplain, she has been to more wakes and has seen more dead bodies than most adults I know. And yet she understands that these deaths are a result of illness, illness that usually occurs over a long course of time, mostly to older people. She is able to walk up to the casket of a stranger, place her little hand on the deceased, and say with the beautiful faith of a cherub, "It's OK. You're with the angels now." Somehow, when she says this, it rings true.

Now she knows that death can come at any time. It can come when parents go to work or when traveling on an airplane. It can come for no reason at all. "Promise me you'll come home," she said, putting her arms around my neck. I was struggling, too. The mother in me felt torn and guilty for leaving, while the chaplain felt anxious to get on my way. Leaving my house was sometimes like ripping off a bandage: the slower the good-byes, the longer it burned.

The kids will be fine, I say to myself. *They will be fine.* It is the truth, as well as a mantra that helps relieve my guilt over leaving them. I try to repeat it enough times to believe it. My husband is home with them and can comfort them if they wake up in the night. I did not dwell on the memory of his face as I left. He, too, had asked if I had to go downtown again. I couldn't tell if he was feeling worried for me, abandoned, or increasingly removed from my life at Ground Zero. I was seeing things that I wasn't sure how to share with him, things I felt he did not *want* me to share, and I was slowly growing withdrawn at the same time. Part of me cried out for his empathy and support, for the opportunity to express the things I was experiencing, while the other part was afraid to voice it—and then hurt at what I perceived as his reluctance to hear. There was also a part, perhaps in both of us, that was in denial about the indelible mark my work at Ground Zero was leaving—on me, on our relationship, and on our children.

I've grown quite adept at packing these thoughts into a nice, neat box whenever I arrive at the Trade Center. My kids, my marriage, my life outside of the morgue can wait for another day. Maybe I am deluding myself that it is service and not some peculiar selfishness that draws me here for each shift. Perhaps it is a mixture of both. All I know is that, for the next eight hours, I will be fully present in the moment. I will step beyond my role as wife and mother toward something closer to a reminder (albeit, a feeble one) of God's compassion and presence.

I suck the cold air into my lungs as the police officer at the checkpoint scans my ID badge and lets me pass. Young soldiers in camouflage stand guard within the perimeter, shifting their weight from one frozen foot to the other. I can't imagine having to stand still in this cold, even in heavy boots. I make sure to thank them for being here, and I encourage them to take advantage of the respite offered at St. Paul's on their break. Besides providing food and hot coffee and a warm place to rest, the church offers massage therapists, chiropractors, a bathroom, and quiet. They respond with a smile and a polite nod, and a glimmer of the boys within the men flickers like lightning beneath the surface; it's there and then gone.

As I continue toward the morgue, the smell of freshly cut wood makes me slow my steps and lift my head. I breathe it in with the same instinctive happiness as I would the aroma of an apple pie. Turning toward the smell, I see the long ramp leading up to an observation deck that is being built for the public. It's scheduled to open in three days, the first of four decks that are planned for the site, allowing the public a closer, unobstructed view of this communal tragedy. Besides seeing the wreckage, they will also bear witness to the work that is being done and the gritty determination of this city to find its dead and to reclaim the space. I am aware that there has been controversy surrounding the observation decks. Some have expressed concern that the Trade Center will become a tourist destination, but in reality, it already has. This doesn't mean that the intentions of the visitors are voyeuristic or disrespectful; they just need to see. It's not unlike the impulse to attend a wake, either out of respect for the living or a need to see the dead in order to believe death is real. I know that I would want to see, if I were not working here. I would feel drawn to this place of pain to pay my respects and to say a prayer.

I continue walking, leaving behind the empty viewing deck that will undoubtedly be filled with people come Sunday, and arrive at the modest trailer that houses the morgue. It is one place where visitors will never be permitted. It's Ground Zero's sacristy. At the far end of the long rectangular room are two stainless-steel receiving tables. They wait patiently, as we all do, for the next remains to be brought in. A couple of EMTs sit in folding chairs talking quietly, a young-looking Port Authority officer leans against the wall, and a detective stretches his back behind a small table. They all glance up when I enter and wave or mumble a hello. A large book rests on the table. Page after page, remnants of the lives that were lost are documented: a foot, an arm, a breast, a bone—the part, the time, the day, the place. When a shift changes, the handwriting changes. It's clear that fewer and smaller remains are being recovered, and it occurs to me that this book, with its detailed findings, is becoming a heartbreaking travelogue about the aftermath of September 11.

For several minutes, I stand there scanning the pages. The neat entries go on and on. I am acutely aware that there is nothing I can do for these bits and particles of people, but I take comfort in the knowledge that someone was there to bless them. Some unnamed colleague, some person of faith, agreed to stand in for the angels and bear witness to a life. Holding the book, I know that I am also holding the prayers that I have prayed. I am holding the bodies over which I have offered blessing—and I shut my eyes for a moment in order to breathe.

As I lay the book back down on the table, the detective yawns and rubs his weary eyes. He tells me that it's been a quiet night. Very few remains have been brought in, which makes the hours pass slowly. At least we have a reprieve from the biting cold. I glance over at the Port Authority officer and recognize him as someone I've met here before—Rudy. He's a tall, powerful-looking man of about twenty-eight years old. His shoulders are broad, and his chest looks like it might pop out of his jacket. Despite his formidable build, Rudy has a sweet face and an easy smile; unlike everyone else in the trailer, he does not look worn out. The contrast is rather striking. I'm curious whether it is his youth or his smooth olive skin that hides any fatigue. My gut tells me his energy is due to something deeper—something in his spirit. The first time I met him here at the morgue, I pointed to the letters on his cap and stupidly asked if he was a police officer from Pennsylvania. "Oh no," he laughed. "PAPD stands for Port Authority Police Department." I was mortified. In the first few weeks of the recovery, I grew accustomed to seeing different letter combinations on caps and jackets because there were so many uniformed personnel from other parts of the country. The most common abbreviations were FDNY and NYPD, but there were plenty of others as well. Rudy had patiently—and proudly—explained to me that members of the PAPD were the first law enforcement personnel to respond to the attacks on September 11. They lost thirty-seven men that day, more officers than any other police department. It occurred to me how much weight he must carry on those broad shoulders—the weight of grief, the weight of surviving, the weight of remembering.

"Hi, Rudy," I say as I walk over to him. "How's Pennsylvania?" Smiling warmly, he extends his hand. "Hey, nice to see you, Rev." In his grip, I can feel his vitality—and I wonder how many other young men and women are represented in that logbook behind me. The thought is almost too much to bear. I ask him how he's been and how he is coping with all the hours he seems to be putting in at the site. Together, we lean against the wall, unconsciously holding back the hurricane of pain that presses against the other side.

"I don't know if I told you this last time," he begins softly, "but one night when I was working here, someone said they thought they'd found remains of one of the hijackers."

His words hit me like a sonic boom. In the last two months, I had heard a lot of stories, both gruesome and heartbreaking. I had stood by while body bags were unzipped. I was aware that fact mingled freely with fiction. But the stories and the people telling them, and the remains we blessed, were all from the perspective of *our* side. This was the first time I'd heard the *other* side mentioned in individual terms. Of course the hijackers' remains had to be mixed in with their victims'; it just hadn't occurred to me, focused as I was on comforting *our* side.

When I ask Rudy why they believed it was one of *them*, he tells me he's not sure but thought it had something to do with where the body was located and its proximity to part of the plane. I picture this body, or part of a body, surrounded by New York City firefighters and cops, by Port Authority officers, and by construction workers who might have lost friends.

"Were you right there?" I ask.

"Yes."

"What did people do when they realized it might be one of the hijackers? Did they spit on the body or desecrate it in any way?" I imagine that the rumor would have ignited some strong emotions, regardless of whether it was true or not.

Without hesitation, Rudy shakes his head. "No . . . not at all. We treated those remains with the same respect as we did all the others." I'm taken aback—it isn't at all what I expected him to say. I marvel at the genuineness of his reaction and the honesty in his voice. I tell him that I am stunned and that I am truly proud of whoever was there at that moment, including him. He looks at me with those clear eyes, as if he couldn't have fathomed any other response. "We just said to each other, hey, remember: this was someone's son. This was still someone's son." I know that I have just heard something holy.

It is almost 2:00 a.m. when I finish my conversation with Rudy and step out of the trailer for some fresh air. No remains have been brought in yet, but I leave my cell phone number on the wall in case this changes. This is the usual procedure. If the night was quiet, morgue chaplains could walk the site and offer support to others. I decide to head toward the firehouse known as Ten House, or 10-10, for Engine Company 10, Ladder Company 10. It is the firehouse that sits at the lip of the site, the closest one to the Trade Center. At the sound of the first plane hitting the North Tower, the men on duty ran to the windows and saw the building on fire. Within hours, five of these men would be dead. The firehouse had been badly damaged but was now being used for storing supplies, among other things. During my shifts, I would often go there to use the bathroom or to stand on the roof and look out at the site. It was a bit eerie inside. Even if I was merely imagining the ghosts of the men hanging about there, I could feel the resonance of their spirits.

As I walk, it dawns on me that things feel different tonight at the site. Something is missing, but I can't put my finger on it. Just before I reach 10-10, I remember: it's the dogs. I am missing the search-and-rescue dogs and the therapy dogs that used to be here. The cold and the lack of recoverable remains, not to mention the fact that I'm working the night shift, have probably kept them away. Their presence was always such a balm to everyone here, myself included. It's amazing what a wagging tail can do to lift the spirit.

When the hope of finding survivors shifted to the hope of finding remains, even the rescue dogs were affected. Day after day, and through the long hours of the night, the dogs searched for life. The constant failure to find any weighed on their spirits. You could see it in their weary eyes and in their postures. Sometimes, to bolster them, a construction worker or a firefighter might cover a fellow worker in some rubble and have the dog handler come near. The dog, catching the scent, would begin digging excitedly for the half-buried person. When this "rescue" was completed, everyone would cheer, and the dog's spirit would be restored. Her tail would wag, her eyes would shine; one could see some inner flame being rekindled. The compassion shown to these dogs resuscitated the spirits of those who were present, reminding them that they had not failed in their missions, either. They were succeeding by having the courage to show up every day, to do the best they could, and to still care about others. We could continue to hope—not that survivors would be found, but that we might survive ourselves.

I am deep in thought about the dogs and about what Rudy told me as I ascend the stairs to the rooftop of 10-10. When I step outside, I am surprised to see another woman standing there, an EMT who looks to be in her late forties. She is leaning over the edge of the wall, her lank blonde hair blowing behind her, reminding me of a figurehead carved at the front of a ship: mysterious, strong, with a face whose emotions are difficult to discern. I am about to leave because I don't want to intrude on her solitude, but she happens to turn and see me there. When our eyes meet, she greets me in a way that is both warm and wary. I've seen similar versions of this expression many times at Ground Zero, so I don't take it personally. I know it is a result of fatigue, sorrow, and the effort it takes to keep emotions under control.

We stand side by side, gazing out as the work goes on without ceasing below us. The boom and grind of the trucks is somewhat muted from our vantage point, absorbed into the acoustic panel of the night sky. The distance from the work and the noise is a relief. We are like birds that have found a high ledge on which to rest.

The EMT tells me how she had arrived just before the second tower fell. "It was like being in hell," she says. "Everything went black. You couldn't breathe. I got separated from my partner in the chaos and darkness. You could hear the screams of people coming from somewhere below your feet, but you couldn't see anything. It was so terrible. I kept thinking of my five kids and just started moving away from the towers. At first I hesitated, thinking I should look for my partner, but then I just kept going. I didn't hear until later that night that he had made it out. If I had gone back for him, I probably wouldn't be here. If he had gone back for me, he wouldn't be, either. He's still too freaked out to come back down here . . . but I come about two or three times a month."

"What do you do with all those images, all those memories?" I ask.

"I don't know," she says. "I guess I just focus on my kids and do what I can to help here."

I would put my life in this woman's hands, I think. She has borne five children, has come face to face with death, and has returned to do it again. For a moment, we stand as mothers, united against a backdrop of sorrow. There are no words. We simply let the bitter wind blow through our hair. Her face is sharp and beautiful, and she looks to me like an angel guarding the site from her post.

"I guess we'd better get back to work," she says. "Maybe I'll see you again."

"I hope so," I reply as I shake her hand. "Take care of those children. They are very lucky to have such a courageous mom."

"Hey, so are yours." She smiles, but then the light behind her eyes dims, as if she's closed the blinds. I don't know if she's retreating back into herself so that she can function or to keep fresh images at bay. It's the part of her story that I will never know.

Descending the stairs, we go our separate ways. I head back to the morgue, and she disappears into the night.

I find myself whispering a prayer after each interaction I have. I mumble silent, wordless petitions—for what? For the safety of these men and women. For their families. For all the families who do not have loved ones coming home anymore. I am praying in order to keep myself moving; I am praying for wisdom, for the right words, for the next person who will need comfort. I am praying that I don't forget the faces of the people I meet. I am braiding them like a prayer shawl around my shoulders.

I walk with long, fast strides back to the trailer, as if I can outrun the cold. Stepping inside, I immediately meet the eyes of an EMS lieutenant. He is a stocky man with gray hair and a baby face. His blue eyes are friendly, though saturated with sadness. I recognize in him what I have seen in countless others here: a shy hunger to tell his story. Until the stories spill from their mouths, many do not know what or how to feel about them. Talking with me or another chaplain is sometimes a way for them to stick their toes back in the water of their emotions, something that can feel frightening to do alone. Sometimes it is a form of confession. I'm not sure what is on the lieutenant's mind, but I can tell he wants to talk.

We move to a corner for some privacy, although we really didn't have to. There are only two other sleepy people in the trailer now, and they appear to be dozing. We begin a casual exchange about home and family. It is always the way things begin. We need to touch base with what makes sense, with the safe and the normal, before we dare venture into the shock and the horror of these days. He tells me about his two children, a boy and a girl. As he describes his son, his eyes start to water and there is a catch in his throat. "He's just such a loving little boy," says the lieutenant. "I can't explain it. He is just so sweet and kind. My daughter is wonderful, too, but she's a handful." He laughs, shaking his head. I sense that he perceives a certain vulnerability in his son that inspires a desire to protect him. Perhaps he yearns to protect him from the dangers faced by so many sons, the dangers that have buried sons just beyond this morgue and on battlefields since, it seems, the beginning of time. If he can protect his son, maybe he can find and protect the child who was brutalized in himself on September 11.

The lieutenant looks at the floor as he wipes his eyes; then he begins to speak of being here on that day. "You can't imagine what it was like. The choices people had to make. The terror. A friend told me how he and his partner had just carried a woman down several flights of stairs in a chair. She was unconscious and looked pretty far gone. As soon as they got outside the building, it began to collapse. You know what they did?" he asked, searching my eyes, searching, searching. "They put her down and just started running. They had to leave the lady there. They knew they only had a few seconds. If they tried to carry her, they all would have died. That poor lady. My friend is still a wreck. He keeps thinking of her. But, you know, he's got four kids. He had to make a choice. And it haunts him. Why should anyone have to make that kind of decision?"

"None of us knows what we would have done in that situation," I say gently. "You can't know until you're in it, and no one has the right to judge anyone else for what they might have done under such life-threatening circumstances."

"You know what the worst part was for me? The dust. Walking through all that dust. We knew we were walking through people's ashes. I was covered in them. Covered with the ashes of other human beings."

The lieutenant begins to cry. He hangs his head and covers his face with his hand, pouring his tears into what feels now like the bottomless cup of our collective sorrow. "I'm sorry," he says, rubbing his eyes. "I haven't cried about this since it happened. I'll be OK." Grief weighs on his sturdy shoulders. He will bear it . . . but will he be OK? Will any of us ever be OK? Despite the odds, there is something about him that gives me hope—his courage, his decency, his tender anguish. I say a silent thanks for his little boy and for his daughter, and I pray for the child in him, the part of him that has been temporarily lost.

Clearly, we choose to come here because we desperately want to help. But what of the images that haunt us? What of the choices from which there is no return? Standing beside the EMS lieutenant, I put my hand on his shoulder. I can feel the angel wings protruding beneath his jacket. Does he know that they are there? Has it occurred to him that the shoes in which he is walking are God's shoes? *Keep talking,* I think. *Keep telling your story. Tell it until your burden is lifted. Tell it until the ashes fall like snowflakes, like forgiveness, dissolving, each one, in unique perfection.*

The winter sun is steadily making its ascent by the time I turn onto my street and pull into the driveway. The houses no longer look like cribs to me; they are the bones that hold us together and keep us from spilling out onto the frosty grass. I need to go into my house, into my body, into my own life again. I want to, but I hesitate for some reason. I know that I am both exhausted and wired; I keep thinking that I've forgotten something. Maybe it's a part of myself and I need to call it back. Maybe I'm overthinking.

The house is quiet as I open the door. Our bulldog, Satch, is snoring loudly on his back; he doesn't even flinch when I walk in, great watchdog that he is. Unwrapped Christmas presents are scattered across the floor—and it feels as if they, too, are sleeping. Only the tree, with its open green arms and perfume of pine, is awake to greet me good morning. I tiptoe up the steps and into my daughter's room; then I stretch out next to her, pressing my nose to her cheek. She smells like warm bread. "Mommy, you're home!" she says sleepily as she snuggles closer.

"Yes, sweetheart, I'm home," I whisper. "I'm home."

I shut my eyes, pulling the curtain on the night. Behind that curtain, machines are still rumbling downtown and fresh workers are replacing the weary. I cannot promise my daughter that I have fulfilled my last shift. The new year is coming, and there is still so much work to be done. I don't have to go again; I could always say no. But I have left fragments of myself at Ground Zero, and I am holding the fragments of others. Until the work is finished, I cannot begin to put myself back together again, and I'm not sure what to do with these other pieces. I have chosen a mosaic of intricate pattern and fragile parts. Even if the picture as a whole is unclear, I know that all the pieces belong there together. The same light refracts through the blues and the whites, the smooth and the jagged. It illuminates the empty places, filling the space until a fragment can be restored. At the moment, I am standing knee deep in shards of colored glass. Perhaps, in time, I will be able to take a step back. And what I hope to discern is a deepening, not a shattering, of faith in humanity, in God, and in the choices I have made.

ACKNOWLEDGMENTS

Immeasurable thanks go to my trusted agent and friend, Cynthia Manson. Meeting you remains one of the great blessings of my life. Thanks also from the bottom of my heart to Amy Hosford and her extraordinary team at Waterfall Press: Sheryl Zajechowski and Andrew Pantoja. Thanks to copyeditor Meredith Tennant and cover designer Joan Wong. Special thanks to editor Caitlin Alexander, whose keen eye and sensitivity to detail continues to make me a better writer.

I am grateful for my mom, who somehow musters the courage to live without my sweet dad, for the childhood my parents provided me and for the faith they inspired. And to my family: thank you for your support, for your encouragement, and for the joy you give me every day. You are my heart.

ABOUT THE AUTHOR

Andrea Raynor, a graduate of Harvard Divinity School, is a United Methodist minister and chaplain. She has been a hospice chaplain since 1997 and is currently serving at Greenwich Hospital Home Hospice in Greenwich, Connecticut. She has worked with the homeless in New York and Boston and was a pastor to churches in New York, Connecticut, and Massachusetts.

In the aftermath of the September 11 attacks, Raynor served as a chaplain in the morgue at Ground Zero, offering both blessings over remains and support to the many workers there. She has lectured throughout the New York area and has appeared as a guest on public television and radio. Raynor is the author of two books: *The Voice That Calls You Home* and *Incognito: Lost and Found at Harvard*. She lives with her family in New York's Westchester County, where she is the chaplain for the Rye Fire Department. Learn more at www.revandrearaynor.com.